Other Books by the Editor

Little House in the Ozarks
"I Remember Laura"
Words from a Fearless Heart

Savir
Grac

Saving Graces

The Inspirational Writings of
Laura Ingalls Wilder

Edited by Stephen Hines

BROADMAN
&HOLMAN
PUBLISHERS

Nashville, Tennessee

Compilation and introduction © 1997 by Stephen W. Hines
Printed in the United States of America
Published by Broadman & Holman Publishers, Nashville, Tennessee

0-8054-0148-2

Dewey Decimal Classification: 242
Subject Heading: DEVOTIONAL LITERATURE / FRONTIER AND PIONEER LIFE
Library of Congress Card Catalog Number: 97-11808

Scriptures are from the King James Version of the Bible.

Library of Congress Cataloging-in-Publication Data
Wilder, Laura Ingalls, 1867–1957.
    Saving graces : the inspirational writings of Laura
Ingalls Wilder / edited by Stephen Hines.
        p.   cm.
    ISBN 0-8054-0148-2
    1. Christian life. 2. Wilder, Laura Ingalls, 1867–1957.
I. Hines, Stephen W. II. Title.
BV4501.2.W51956 1997
813'.52—dc21   97-11808
                                                              CIP

                1 2 3 4 5 01 00 99 98 97

Contents

Contents

Acknowledgments

I wish to thank the staff at the Lila D. Bunch Library at Belmont University in Nashville for their kind assistance in helping me find hymns for *Saving Graces*.

Also, my thanks to Matthew Jacobson of Broadman and Holman for believing in this project and adding so materially to it.

Finally, my thanks to my family for enduring my many closeted moments in my study.

Introduction: The Christian Faith of Laura Ingalls Wilder

One of the happiest discoveries I made when I first began to research the adult writings of renowned children's author Laura Ingalls Wilder was the genuineness of her Christian faith. I knew, of course, that her family had been religious, both from her autobiographical writings and from the television show based on her life, "Little House on the Prairie." But because there is such a thing as literary license, and because it was beginning to become known that her daughter had helped with the writing of her famous books, I was truly surprised at the openness of Mrs. Wilder's Christian convictions in her later writings.

For my book *"I Remember Laura,"* I interviewed Mrs. Iola Jones, one of Mrs. Wilder's many friends. I learned that Laura had memorized long sections of Scripture and that, although she had been inactive in church since the death of her husband, Almanzo, she was delighted to begin receiving rides to church from the Joneses, a neighboring family. Others remembered that Laura often kept a Bible close at hand during those years after her husband's death.

However, Mrs. Wilder did not discover religion late in life as some sort of grief-filled consolation—quite the contrary. According to one of her close friends who helped get Laura to the local Methodist church in Mansfield, Missouri, her Christian faith had a long history, dating from her conversion as a child in Burr Oak, Iowa.

Many people will be surprised to learn that the Ingalls family ever lived in Iowa. No mention of the family's approximate two-year stay in Burr Oak, where the family helped run a hotel, is made in her children's books, and no one knows quite sure why. It is possible, however, that the family's time in Burr Oak may have been the worst point of the Ingallses' prairie pilgrimage. There was a sense of desperation about the family's future that Laura had never experienced before. Pa was as close to broke as he had ever been, and Ma had seen their only son die just a few months before. There were doctor bills to pay and grieving to do, all at the same time.

During the midst of this wilderness experience, Laura knelt to pray one evening with an especially heavy burden on her heart for her parents and the whole desperate situation. As she poured out her heart to God, Laura was filled with an overwhelming feeling, undoubtedly the presence of the Almighty, and she thought to herself, *This is what men call God!* Even though the moment passed quickly, her faith was renewed, and the family began the slow process to financial recovery.

Despite Laura's spiritual renewal, her religious life was not without doubts or disappointments. Religion on the frontier could be pretty harsh. Monitory preaching was then the practice, and some ministers preached a repentance so dramatic that almost anyone would wonder if such a thing could happen to them. Mrs. Wilder continually described her favorite religious people as mild-mannered.

Laura attended both Congregational and Methodist services, providing quite a contrast of approaches to Christian ideals. The early

Congregational home mission works were somewhat like independent evangelical churches of today in that they emphasized unity in Christ and downplayed traditionally controversial topics like the Lord's Supper and baptism. If they were the only church in a new settlement, they tried to accommodate as many people as possible. On the other hand, the Methodists were active in evangelizing the West; a Methodist congregation was likely to sprout up wherever their zeal was wanted. Their strong temperance message was also popular among western settlers.

Laura fellowshipped with the Methodists on Wednesdays and with the Congregationalists on Sundays. Officially, her family were members of the Congregationalist church and helped found the church in Walnut Grove, Minnesota, but the Methodists gave Laura a much-appreciated outlet for her singing. Because Laura liked singing so much, I have included some hymns that were popular in Laura's time, many of which she sang during those Sunday and Wednesday services.

In addition to the singing that took place at services, there were also testimonies, a part of worship about which Laura was less enthusiastic. Testimonies—at least as she experienced them—often made her uncomfortable. Laura was shy, and such public expressions may have shocked her. She once told a friend years later, "Of course you loved God, but you also loved your mother, and somehow it didn't seem quite right to go around bragging about it." Perhaps she was raised hearing "bragamonies" rather than testimonies, but in any case, her Christian life had its firm foundations in her devout family, her church, and her God.

It was this background that prepared Laura Ingalls Wilder for one of her life's greatest opportunities: to become the home department writer for a farm newspaper circulated to some 100,000 people throughout Missouri. From this platform, Mrs. Wilder was able to record the lessons she had learned from family, friends, and her personal experience with God. These lessons in living constitute her legacy of faith for us today and comprise the sum and substance of this book.

Can a woman who was born in 1867 and who died in 1957 have anything worthwhile to say to us today? My assertion is a resounding yes! No matter what changes the times may bring, there are only so many lessons to be learned in life, and these same lessons seem to keep emerging from generation to generation—sometimes taught by the hard experience of trial and error, and other times through the mercy of a lesson from someone whose wise words we accept and apply to our own lives.

As radio personality Paul Harvey is reported to have said, "It is a good thing to know that in times like these there have always been times like these." If you doubt this truth, please read on and judge for yourself. You'll be amazed at what Laura has to teach you.

Rock of Ages, Cleft for Me 163

1. Rock of A-ges, cleft for me, Let me hide my-self in thee;
2. Not the la-bors of my hands Can ful-fill thy law's de-mands;
3. While I draw this fleet-ing breath, When mine eyes shall close in death,

Let the wa-ter and the blood, From thy wound-ed side which flowed,
Could my zeal no res-pite know, Could my tears for-ev-er flow,
When I rise to worlds un-known, And be-hold thee on thy throne,

Be of sin the dou-ble cure, Save from wrath and make me pure.
All for sin could not a-tone; Thou must save, and thou a-lone.
Rock of A-ges, cleft for me, Let me hide my-self in thee. A-MEN.

Psalm 94:22. Words, Augustus M. Toplady, 1775, 1776. Tune TOPLADY, Thomas Hastings, 1832.

Compass Needle to the Star

Out in the meadow, I picked a wild sunflower, and as I looked into its golden heart, such a wave of homesickness came over me that I almost wept. I wanted Mother, with her gentle voice and quiet firmness; I longed to hear Father's jolly songs and to see his twinkling blue eyes; I was lonesome for the sister with whom I used to play in the meadow picking daisies and wild sunflowers.

Across the years, the old home and its love called to me and memories of sweet words of counsel came flooding back. I realize that all my life the teachings of those early days have influenced me, and the example set by Father and Mother has been something I have tried to follow, with failures here and there, with rebellion at times; but always coming back to it as the compass needle to the star.

> *Who can find a virtuous woman? for her price is far above rubies. . . . Strength and honour are her clothing; and she shall rejoice in time to come. She openeth her mouth with wisdom: and in her tongue is the law of kindness. She looketh well to the ways of her household, and eateth not the bread of idleness. Her children arise up, and call her blessed; her husband also, and he praiseth her. Many daughters have done virtuously, but thou excellest them all. Favour is deceitful, and beauty is vain: but a woman that feareth the LORD, she shall be praised.*
> —PROVERBS 31:10; 25–30

So much depends upon the homemakers. I sometimes wonder if they are so busy now with other things that they are forgetting the importance of this special work. Especially did I wonder when reading recently that there were a great many child suicides in the United States during the last year. Not long ago we never had heard of such a thing in our own country, and I am sure that there must be something wrong with the home of a child who commits suicide.

Because of their importance, we must not neglect our homes in the rapid changes of the present day. For when tests of character come in later years, strength to the good will not come from the modern improvements or amusements few may have enjoyed, but from the quiet moments and the "still small voices" of the old home. Nothing ever can take the place of this early home influence; and as it does not depend on externals, it may be the possession of the poor as well as the rich, a heritage from all fathers and mothers to their children.

The real things of life that are the common possession of us all are of the greatest value—worth far more than motor cars or radios, more than lands or money—and our whole store of these wonderful riches may be revealed to us by such a common, beautiful thing as a wild sunflower.

Success?

I was told to go into a certain community and get the story of the most successful person in it.

"There are no successes there," I said, "just ordinary people, not one of whom has contributed to the progress of the world. I can get no story there worth anything as an inspiration to others."

Then came the reply: "Surely someone has lived a clean life, has good friends, and the love of family. Such a one must have contributed something of good to others."

And he looked up, and saw the rich men casting their gifts into the treasury. And he saw also a certain poor widow casting in thither two mites. And he said, Of a truth I say unto you, that this poor widow hath cast in more than they all: For all these have of their abundance cast in unto the offerings of God: but she of her penury hath cast in all the living that she had.

—LUKE 21:1–4

Rearranging my standard of "success" to include something besides accumulated wealth—achieved ambition of a spectacular sort—I thought of Grandma and Grandpa Culver, poor as church mice, but a fine old couple, loved by everybody and loving everybody. Home meant something to their children who return there year after year. I went to see them.

"No," Grandma told me over the jelly she was making for the sick, "Pa and I never have been well-off in money, but oh, so very rich in love of each other, of family, and of friends.

"We've tried to see every little submerged virtue in each other, in the children, and in everybody. I had the gift of cheerfulness; Pa had patience; we cultivated these traits.

"Every day we have tried to be of a little use to somebody, never turning down a single opportunity to help someone to a glimpse of things worthwhile. What we have lacked in money and brilliance, we have tried to make up in service."

But ever the world has let the flash of more dazzling successes blind it to the value of such lives as these.

Putting First Things First

Some small boys went into my neighbor's yard this spring [1922] and with sling shots killed the wild birds that were nesting there. Only the other day, I read in my daily paper of several murders committed by a nineteen-year-old boy.

At once there was formed a connection in my mind between the two crimes, for both were crimes of the same kind, though perhaps in differing degree—the breaking of laws and the taking of life cruelly.

For the cruel child to become a hard-hearted boy and then a brutal man is only stepping along the road on which he has started. A child allowed to disobey without punishment is not likely to have much respect for law as he grows older. Not that every child who kills birds becomes a murderer, nor that everyone who is not taught to obey goes to prison.

The Bible says, "Train up a child in the way he should go: and when he is old, he will not depart from it" [Prov. 22:6]. The opposite is also true, and if a child is started in the way he should not go, he will go at least some way along that road as he grows older. It will always be more difficult for him to travel the right way even though he finds it.

> *For ever, O LORD, thy word is settled in heaven. Thy faithfulness is unto all generations: thou hast established the earth, and it abideth. They continue this day according to thine ordinances: for all are thy servants. Unless thy law had been my delights, I should then have perished in mine affliction. I will never forget thy precepts: for with them thou hast quickened me. I am thine, save me; for I have sought thy precepts. The wicked have waited for me to destroy me: but I will consider thy testimonies. I have seen an end of all perfection: but thy commandment is exceeding broad.*
> —PSALM 119:89–96

The first laws with which children come in contact are the commands of their parents. Few fathers and mothers are wise in giving these, for we are all so busy and thoughtless. But I am sure we will all agree that these laws of ours should be as wise and as few as possible, and, once given, children should be made to obey or shown that to disobey brings punishment. Thus they will learn the lesson every good citizen and every good man and woman learns sooner or later—that breaking a law brings suffering.

If we break a law of nature, we are punished physically; when we disobey God's law we suffer spiritually, mentally, and usually in our bodies also; man's laws, being founded on the Ten Commandments, are really mankind's poor attempt at interpreting the laws of God, and for disobeying them there is a penalty. The commands we give our children should be our translation of these laws of God and man, founded on justice and the law of love, which is the Golden Rule.

And these things enter into such small deeds. Even insisting that children pick up and put away their playthings is teaching them order, the law of the universe, and helpfulness, the expression of love.

The responsibility for starting the child in the right way is the parents'—it cannot be delegated to the schools or to the state, for the little feet start on life's journey from the home.

Let Us Be Just

Two little girls had disagreed, as was to be expected because they were so temperamentally different. They wanted to play in different ways, and as they had to play together, all operations were stopped while they argued the question. The elder of the two had a sharp tongue and great facility in using it. The other was slow to speak but quick to act and they both did their best according to their abilities.

Said the first little girl: "You've got a snub nose and your hair is just a common brown color. I heard Aunt Lottie say so! Ah, don't you wish your hair was a b-e-a-u-tiful golden like mine and your nose a fine shape? Cousin Louisa said that about me. I heard her!"

The second little girl could not deny these things. Her dark skin, brown hair, and snub nose, as compared with her sister's lighter coloring and regular features, were a tragedy in her life. She could think of nothing cutting to reply for she was not given to saying unkind things nor was her tongue nimble enough to say them, so she stood digging her bare toes into the ground, hurt, helpless, and tongue-tied.

The first girl, seeing the effect of her words, talked on. "Besides, you're two years younger than I am, and I know more than you, so you have to mind me and do as I say!"

This was too much! Sister was prettier; no answer could be made to that. She was older, it could not be denied; but that gave her no right to command. At last, here was a chance to act!

"And you have to mind me," repeated the first little girl.

"I will not!" said the second little girl, and then, to show her utter contempt for such authority, this little brown girl slapped her elder, golden-haired sister.

I hate to write the end of the story. No, not the end! No story is ever ended! It goes on and on, and the effects of this one followed this little girl all her life, showing her hatred of injustice. I should say that I dislike to tell what came next, for the golden-haired sister ran crying and told what had happened, except her own part in the quarrel, and the little brown girl was severely punished. To be plain, she was soundly spanked and set in a corner. She did not cry but sat glowering at the parent who punished her and thinking in her rebellious little mind that when she was large enough, she would return the spanking with interest.

It was not the pain of the punishment that hurt so much as the sense of injustice, the knowledge that she had not been treated fairly by one from whom she had the right to expect fair treatment, and that there had been a failure to understand where she had thought a mistake impossible. She had been beaten and bruised by her sister's unkind words and had been unable to reply. She had defended herself in the only way possible for her and felt that she had a perfect right to do so, or if not, then both should have been punished.

And as ye would that men should do to you, do ye also to them likewise.

—Luke 6:31

Children have a fine sense of justice that sometimes is far truer than that of older persons, and in almost every case, if appealed to, will prove the best help in governing them. When children are ruled through their sense of justice, there are no angry thoughts left to rankle in their minds. Then a punishment is not an injury inflicted upon them by someone who is larger and stronger but the inevitable consequence of their own acts, and a child's mind will understand this much sooner than one would think. What a help all their lives in self-control and self-government this kind of a training would be!

We are prone to put so much emphasis on the desirability of mercy that we overlook the beauties of the principle of justice. The quality of mercy is a gracious, beautiful thing; but with more justice in the world, there would be less need for mercy, and exact justice is most merciful in the end.

The difficulty is that we are so likely to make mistakes, we cannot trust our judgment and so must be merciful to offset our own shortcomings; but I feel sure when we are able to comprehend the workings of the principle of justice, we shall find that instead of being opposed to each other, infallible justice and mercy are one and the same thing.

468 When I Can Read My Title Clear

PISGAH. 8. 6. 8. 6. 6. 6. 8. 6.

ISAAC WATTS, 1674-1748   J. C. LOWRY, 1820-?

1. When I can read my ti - tle clear To man-sions in the skies,
2. Should earth a - gainst my soul en - gage, And fier - y darts be hurled,
3. Let cares, like a wild del - uge come, And storms of sor - row fall!
4. There shall I bathe my wea - ry soul In seas of heav'n-ly rest,

I'll bid fare-well to ev - 'ry fear, And wipe my weep - ing eyes;
Then I can smile at Sa - tan's rage, And face a frown - ing world;
May I but safe - ly reach my home, My God, my heav'n, my all;
And not a wave of trou - ble roll A - cross my peace - ful breast;

And wipe my weep - ing eyes, And wipe my weep - ing eyes,
And face a frown-ing world, And face a frown - ing world,
My God, my heav'n, my all, My God, my heav'n, my all,
A - cross my peace - ful breast, A - cross my peace - ful breast,

I'll bid fare-well to ev - 'ry fear, And wipe my weep - ing eyes.
Then I can smile at Sa - tan's rage, And face a frown - ing world.
May I but safe - ly reach my home, My God, my heav'n, my all.
And not a wave of trou - ble roll A - cross my peace - ful breast.

Why Is the World So Beautiful If Not for Us?

King Winter has sent warning of his coming! There was a delightful freshness in the air the other morning [1916], and all over the low places lay the first frost of the season.

What a beautiful world this is! Have you noticed the wonderful coloring of the sky at sunrise? For me there is no time like the early morning, when the spirit of light broods over the earth at its awakening. What glorious colors in the woods these days! Did you ever think that great painters have spent their lives trying to reproduce on canvas what we may see every day?

Thousands of dollars are paid for their pictures which are not so beautiful as those nature gives us freely. The colors in the sky at sunset, the delicate tints of the early spring foliage, the brilliant autumn leaves, the softly-colored grasses and lovely flowers—what painter ever equaled their beauties with paint and brush?

> *When I consider thy heavens, the work of thy fingers,*
> *the moon and the stars, which thou hast ordained;*
> *what is man, that thou art mindful of him? and the*
> *son of man, that thou visitest him? For thou hast made*
> *him a little lower than the angels, and hast crowned*
> *him with glory and honour.*
>
> —PSALM 8:3–5

I have in my living room three large windows uncovered by curtains which I call my pictures. Ever changing with the seasons, with wild birds and gay squirrels passing on and off the scene, I never have seen a landscape painting to compare with them.

As we go about our daily tasks the work will seem lighter if we enjoy these beautiful things that are just outside our doors and windows. It pays to go to the top of the hill now and then to see the view and to stroll thru the woodlot or pasture forgetting that we are in a hurry or that there is such a thing as a clock in the world. You are "so busy!" Oh, yes, I know it! We are all busy, but what are we living for anyway, and why is the world so beautiful if not for us? The habits we form last us through this life, and I firmly believe into the next. Let's not make such a habit of hurry and work that when we leave this world, we will feel impelled to hurry through the spaces of the universe using our wings for feather dusters to clean away the star dust.

The true way to live is to enjoy every moment as it passes, and surely it is in the everyday things around us that the beauty of life lies.

> I strolled today down a woodland path—
> A crow cawed loudly and flew away.
> The sky was blue and the clouds were gold
> And drifted before me fold on fold;
> The leaves were yellow and red and brown
> And patter, patter the nuts fell down,

On this beautiful, golden autumn day.
A squirrel was storing his winter hoard,
The world was pleasant: I lingered long,
The brown quails rose with a sudden whirr
And a little bundle, of eyes and fur,
Took shape of a rabbit and leaped away.
A little chipmunk came out to play
And the autumn breeze sang a wonder song.

Heavenly Blessings without Number

The older we grow the more precious become the recollections of childhood's days, especially our memories of mother. Her love and care halo her memory with a brighter radiance, for we have discovered that nowhere else in the world is such loving self-sacrifice to be found; her counsels and instructions appeal to us with greater force than when we received them because our knowledge of the world and our experience of life have proved their worth.

The pity of it is that it is by our own experience we have had to gain this knowledge of their value; then when we have learned it in the hard school of life, we know that mother's words were true. So, from generation to generation, the truths of life are taught by precept, and, generation after generation, we each must be burned by fire before we will admit the truth that it will burn.

> *Greatly desiring to see thee, being mindful of thy tears, that I may be filled with joy; when I call to remembrance the unfeigned faith that is in thee, which dwelt first in thy grandmother Lois, and thy mother Eunice; and I am persuaded that [is] in thee also. Wherefore I put thee in remembrance that thou stir up the gift of God, which is in thee by the putting on of my hands.*
> —2 TIMOTHY 1:4–6

We would be saved some sorry blunders and many a heart-ache if we might begin our knowledge where our parents leave off instead of experimenting for ourselves, but life is not that way.

Still, mother's advice does help, and often a word of warning spoken years before will recur to us at just the right moment to save us a misstep. And lessons learned at mother's knee last thru life.

But dearer even than mother's teachings are little, personal memories of her, different in each case but essentially the same—mother's face, mother's touch, mother's voice:

> Childhood's far days were full of joy,
> So merry and bright and gay;
> On sunny wings of happiness
> Swiftly they flew away.
> But oh! By far the sweetest hour
> Of all the whole day long
> Was the slumber hour at twilight
> And my mother's voice in song—
> "Hush, my babe; be still and slumber,
> Holy angels guard thy bed,
> Heavenly blessings without number
> Gently resting on thy head."
> Though our days are filled with gladness,
> Joys of life like sunshine fall;

Still life's slumber hour at twilight
May be sweetest of them all.
And when to realms of boundless peace,
I am waiting to depart
Then my mother's song at twilight
Will make music in my heart.
"Hush, my babe, lie still and slumber;
Holy angels guard thy bed."
And I'll fall asleep so sweetly,
Mother's blessings on my head.

Forgetting Those Things Which Are Behind

Did you ever hear anyone say, "I don't know what the world is coming to"; "People didn't used to do that way"; "Things were different when I was young," or words to that effect?

Is it possible you ever said anything of the kind yourself? If so, don't be deluded into thinking it is because of your knowledge of life nor that the idea is at all original with you. That remark has become a habit with the human race, having been made at least nine hundred years ago, and I suspect it has been repeated by every generation.

An interesting article in *Asia* [1921] tells of a book of old Japan that is being translated by the great Japanese scholars, Mr. Aston and Mr. Sansome. The book was written by a lady of the court, during the reign of the Japanese Emperor Ichijo nearly a thousand years ago.

Among other interesting things in the article, I found this quotation from the old book: "'In olden times,' said one of her Majesty's ladies, 'even the common people had elegant tastes. You never hear of such things nowadays.'"

Doesn't that have a familiar sound? One's mind grows dizzy trying to imagine what things would have been like in the times that were "olden times" a thousand years ago, but evidently things were "going from bad to worse" even then.

"Distance lends enchantment to the view," looking in one direction as well as in another, and that is why, I think, events of olden times and of our childhood and youth are enveloped in such a rosy cloud, just as at the time the future glowed with bright colors. It all depends on which way we're looking. Youth ever gazes forward while age is inclined to look back. And so older persons think things were better when they were young.

Not long ago, I caught myself saying, "When I was a child, children were more respectful to their parents"; when as a matter of fact, I can remember children who were not so obedient as some who are with us today; and I know, when I am truthful with myself, that it always, as now, has taken all kinds of children to make the world.

Sometimes we are inclined to wish our childhood days might come again, but I am always rescued from such folly by remembering a remark I once heard a man make: "Wish I were a boy again," he exclaimed, "I do not! When I was a boy I had to hoe my row in the cornfield with father and the hired man; I must keep up too, and then while they rested in the shade I had to run and get the drinking water."

And so quite often the rather morbid longing for the past will be dispelled by facing the plain facts.

There are abuses in the world, today, surely; there have always been. Our job is to face those of our day and correct them.

We have been doing a great deal of howling over the high prices we have to pay and the comparatively low prices we get [for farm produce], and we should do more than cry aloud about it, but we would have suffered worse in those good old times after the Civil War when the coarsest of muslin and calico cost fifty cents a yard and banks failed overnight leaving their worthless money in circulation.

Prices have not been so high after this much greater war [WW 1], and our money has been good. It is a frightful thing that our civilization should be disgraced by the conditions of the world today, but in the former Dark Ages of history there was no Red Cross organization working to help and save.

Abuses there are, to be sure, wrongs to be righted, sorrows to be comforted; these are obstacles to be met and overcome. But as far back as I can remember, the old times were good times; they have been good all down thru the years, full of love and service, of ideals and achievement—the future is in our hands to make it what we will.

> *Not as though I had already attained, either were already perfect: but I follow after, if that I may apprehend that for which also I am apprehended of Christ Jesus. Brethren, I count not myself to have apprehended: but this one thing I do, forgetting those things which are behind, and reaching forth unto those things which are before, I press toward the mark for the prize of the high calling of God in Christ Jesus.*
> —PHILIPPIANS 3:12–14

Love and service, with a belief in the future and expectation of better things in the tomorrow of the world is a good working philosophy; much better than, "in olden times—things were so much better when I was young." For there is no turning back nor standing still; we must go forward, into the future, generation after generation toward the accomplishment of the ends that have been set for the human race.

However fleeting and changeable life may appear to be on the surface, we know that the great underlying values of life are always the same; no different today than they were a thousand years ago.

Amazing Grace! How Sweet the Sound 165

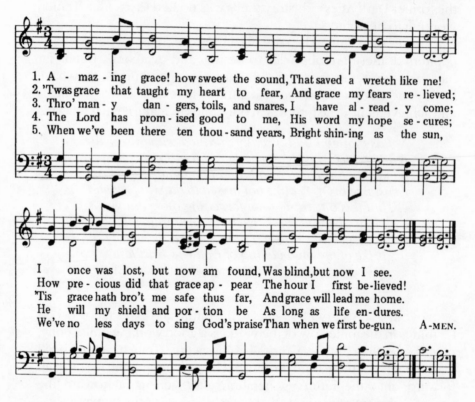

1. A - maz - ing grace! how sweet the sound, That saved a wretch like me!
2. 'Twas grace that taught my heart to fear, And grace my fears re - lieved;
3. Thro' man - y dan - gers, toils, and snares, I have al - read - y come;
4. The Lord has prom - ised good to me, His word my hope se - cures;
5. When we've been there ten thou - sand years, Bright shin - ing as the sun,

I once was lost, but now am found, Was blind, but now I see.
How pre - cious did that grace ap - pear The hour I first be - lieved!
'Tis grace hath bro't me safe thus far, And grace will lead me home.
He will my shield and por - tion be As long as life en - dures.
We've no less days to sing God's praise Than when we first be - gun. A -MEN.

Words, st. 1-4, John Newton, 1779; st. 5, Anonymous. Tune AMAZING GRACE, *Virginia Harmony*, 1831; arranged, Edwin O. Excell, 1900.

A Fool's Prayer

Among my books of verse, there is an old poem that I could scarcely do without. It is "The Fool's Prayer" by Edward Rowland Sill, and every now and then I have been impelled in deep humiliation of spirit to pray the prayer made by that old-time jester of the king.

Even though one is not in the habit of making New Year's resolutions, to be broken whenever the opportunity arises, still, as the old year departs [1918], like Lot's wife, we cannot resist a backward glance. As we see in retrospect, the things we have done that we ought not and the things we have left undone that we should have done, we have a hope that the coming year will show a better record.

In my glance backward and hope for the future, one thing became plain to me—that I valued the love and appreciation of my friends more than ever before, and that I would try to show my love for them, that I would be more careful of their feelings, more tactful, and so endear myself to them.

> *Let love be without dissimulation. Abhor that which is evil; cleave to that which is good. Be kindly affectioned one to another with brotherly love; in honour preferring one another.*
>
> —ROMANS 12:9–10

A few days later a friend and I went together to an afternoon gathering where refreshments were served, and we came back to my friend's home just as the evening meal was ready. The Man of the Place failed to meet me and so I stayed unexpectedly. My friend made apologies for the simple meal, and I said that I preferred plain food to such as we had in the afternoon, which was the same as saying that her meal was plain and that the afternoon refreshments had been finer. I felt that I had said the wrong thing, and in a desperate effort to make amends, I praised the soup which had been served. Not being satisfied to let well enough alone, because of my embarrassment I continued, "It is so easy to have delicious soups, one can make them of just any little things that are left."

And all the way home as I rode quietly beside the Man of the Place I kept praying "The Fool's Prayer": "O Lord, be merciful to me, a fool."

We can afford to laugh at a little mistake such as that, however embarrassing it may be. To laugh and forget is one of the saving graces, but only a little later I was guilty of another mistake over which I could not laugh.

Mrs. G and I were in a group of women at a social affair; but having a little business to talk over, we stepped into another room where we were almost immediately followed by an acquaintance. We greeted her and then went on with our conversation, from which she was excluded. I forgot her presence, and then I looked her way again; she was gone. We had not been kind, and to make it worse, she was comparatively a stranger among us.

In a few minutes everyone was leaving without my having had a chance to make amends in any way. I could not apologize without giving a point to the rudeness, but I thought that I would be especially gracious to her when we met again so she would not feel that we made her an outsider. Now I learn that it will be months before I see her again. I know that she is very sensitive and that I must have hurt her. Again and from the bottom of my heart, I prayed "The Fool's Prayer":

> These clumsy feet, still in the mire,
> Go crushing blossoms without end;
> These hard, well-meaning hands we thrust
> Among the heart-strings of a friend—
> O Lord, be merciful to me, a fool.

As we grow old enough to have a proper perspective, we see such things work out to their conclusion or rather to a partial conclusion, for the effects go on and on endlessly. Very few of our misdeeds are with deliberate intent to do wrong. Our hearts are mostly in the right place, but we seem to be weak in the head.

> 'Tis not by guilt the onward sweep
> Of truth and right, O Lord, we stay;
> 'Tis by our follies that so long
> We hold the earth from heaven away.
> Our faults no tenderness should ask;
> The chastening stripes must cleanse them all;
> But for our blunder—oh, in shame
> Before the eyes of heaven we fall.

Without doubt each one of us is fully entitled to pray the whole of "The Fool's Prayer" and more especially the refrain: "O Lord, be merciful to me, a fool."

Honor and Duty

"Now can we depend on you in this?" asked Mr. Jones. "Certainly you can," replied Mr. Brown. "I'll do it!"

"But you failed us before, you know," continued Mr. Jones, "and it made us a lot of trouble. How would it be for you to put up a forfeit? Will you put up some money as security that you will not fail; will you bet on it?"

"No-o-o," answered Mr. Brown. "I won't bet on it, but I'll give you my word of honor."

How much was Mr. Brown's word worth? I would not want to risk much on it. Would you?

He evidently considered it of less value than a little cash. Now and then we hear of people whose word is as good as their bond, but far too often we find that "word of honor" is used carelessly and then forgotten or ignored.

> *Again, ye have heard that it hath been said by them of old time, Thou shalt not forswear thyself, but shalt perform unto the Lord thine oaths: but I say unto you, Swear not at all . . . neither by Jerusalem; for it is the city of the great King. Neither shalt thou swear by thy head, because thou canst not make one hair white or black. But let your communication be, Yea, yea; Nay, nay: for whatsoever is more than these cometh of evil.*
> —MATTHEW 5:33–37

Speaking to a friend of the difficulties of putting thru a plan we had in mind, I remarked that it was very difficult to do anything with a crowd any more, for so many would promise and then fail to keep the promise.

"I know," she replied, "I do that way myself; it is so much easier to say 'yes,' and then do as I please afterward."

If my friend had realized how weak and unkind her reason was for disregarding her word, she would be more careful, for she prides herself on her strength of character and is a very kind, lovable woman on the whole.

Mr. Brown and my friend had mistaken ideas of value. One's word is of infinitely more worth than money. If money is lost, more money, and just as good, is to be had; but if you pledge your word and do not redeem it, you have lost something that cannot be replaced. It is intangible perhaps but nevertheless valuable to you.

A person who cannot be depended upon by others, in time, becomes unable to depend upon himself. It seems in some subtle way to undermine and weaken the character when we do not hold ourselves strictly responsible for what we say.

And what a tangle it makes of all our undertakings when people do not keep their promises. How much pleasanter it would be, and how much more would be accomplished, if we did not give our word unless we intended to keep it, so that we would all know what we could depend upon!

When we think of honor we always think of duty in connection with it. They seem to be inseparably linked together. The following incident illustrates this.

Albert Bebe, a French resident of San Francisco, came home from the battlefront [WW 1] in France. He had been in the trenches for two years and four months in an advanced position, a "listening post" only sixty yards from the German trenches. Marie Bebe, the soldier's little daughter, was very much excited over her father's coming and objected to going to school the next morning. She thought she should be allowed to stay at home on the first day of her father's visit.

But her mother said: "No! Your father went to fight for France because it was his duty to go. You must go to school because that is your duty. Your father did his duty and you must do yours!" And Marie went to school.

If everybody did his duty as well in the smaller things, there would be no failures when the greater duties presented themselves.

What Comes Out of the Heart

A wonderful way has been invented to transform a scene on the stage, completely changing the apparent surroundings of the actors and their costumes without moving an article. The change is made in an instant. By an arrangement of light and colors, the scenes are so painted that with a red light thrown upon them, certain parts come into view while other parts remain invisible. By changing a switch and throwing a blue light upon the scene, what has been visible disappears and things unseen before appear, completely changing the appearance of the stage.

This late achievement of science is a good illustration of a fact we all know but so easily forget or overlook—that things and persons appear to us according to the light we throw upon them from our own minds.

> *And when he had called all the people unto him, he said unto them, Hearken unto me every one of you, and understand: there is nothing from without a man, that entering into him can defile him: but the things which come out of him, those are they that defile the man.*
>
> —MARK 7:14–15

When we are down-hearted and discouraged, we speak of looking at the world through blue glasses; nothing looks the same to us; our family and friends do not appear the same; our home and work show in the darkest colors. But when we are happy, we see things in a brighter light and everything is transformed.

How unconsciously we judge others by the light that is within ourselves, condemning or approving them by our own conception of right and wrong, honor and dishonor! We show by our judgment just what the light within us is. What we see is always affected by the light in which we look at it so that no two persons see people and things alike. What we see and how we see depends upon the nature of our light.

A quotation, the origin of which I have forgotten, lingers in my mind: "You cannot believe in honor until you have achieved it. Better keep yourself clean and bright; you are the window through which you must see the world."

To Appreciate Heaven

"One gains a lot by going out into the world, by traveling and living in different places," Rose [Mrs. Wilder's daughter] said to me one day, "but one loses a great deal, too. After all, I'm not sure but the loss is greater than the gain."

"Just how do you mean?" I asked.

"I mean this," said Rose. "The best anyone can get out of this world is happiness and contentment, and people here in the country seem so happy and contented, so different from the restless people of the cities who are out in the rush of things."

So after all, there are compensations. Though we do not have the advantages of travel, we stay-at-homes may acquire a culture of the heart that is almost impossible in the rush and roar of cities.

I think there are always compensations. The trouble is we do not recognize them. We usually are so busily longing for things we can't have that we overlook what we have in their place that is even more worthwhile. Sometimes we realize our happiness only by comparison after we have lost it. It really appears to be true that

> To appreciate Heaven well
> A man must have some 15 minutes of Hell.

Talking with another friend from the city gave me still more of an understanding of this difference between country and city.

"My friends in town always are going somewhere. They never are quiet a minute if they can help it," he said. "Always they are looking for something to pass the time away quickly as though they were afraid to be left by themselves. The other evening one of the fellows was all broken up because there was nothing doing. 'There isn't a thing on for tonight,' he said. 'Not a thing!' He seemed to think it was something terrible that there was nothing special on hand for excitement, and he couldn't bear to think of spending a quiet evening at home."

> *Not that I speak in respect of want: for I have learned,*
> *in whatsoever state I am, therewith to be content. I*
> *know both how to be abased, and I know how to*
> *abound: every where and in all things I am instructed*
> *both to be full and to be hungry, both to abound and*
> *to suffer need.*
>
> —PHILIPPIANS 4:11–12

What an uncomfortable condition to be in—depending altogether on things outside of one's self for happiness and a false happiness at that, for the true must come from within.

If we are such bad company that we can't live with ourselves, something is seriously wrong and should be attended to, for sooner or later we shall have to face ourselves alone.

There seems to be a madness in the cities, a frenzy in the struggling crowds. A friend writes me of New York, "I like it and I hate it. There's something you've got to love, it's so big—a people hurrying everywhere, all trying to live and be someone or something—and then, when you see the poverty and hatefulness, the uselessness of it all, you wonder why people live here at all. It does not seem possible that there are any peaceful farms on the earth."

And so more than ever I am thankful for the peacefulness and comparative isolation of country life. This is a happiness which we ought to realize and enjoy.

We who live in the quiet places have the opportunity to become acquainted with ourselves, to think our own thoughts, and live our own lives in a way that is not possible for those who are keeping up with the crowd, where there is always something "on for tonight," and who have become so accustomed to crowds that they are dependent upon them for comfort.

> In thine own cheerful spirit live,
> Nor seek the calm that others give;
> For thou, thyself, alone must stand
> Not held upright by other's hand.

302   A Shelter in the Time of Storm

Words arranged

Ira D. Sankey

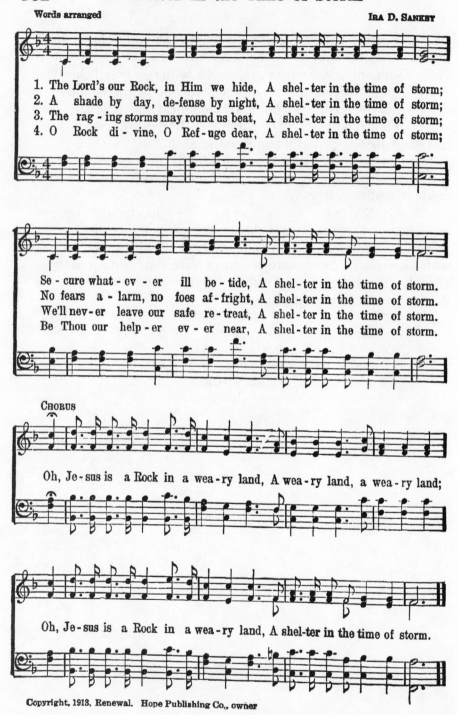

1. The Lord's our Rock, in Him we hide, A shel-ter in the time of storm;
2. A shade by day, de-fense by night, A shel-ter in the time of storm;
3. The rag-ing storms may round us beat, A shel-ter in the time of storm;
4. O Rock di-vine, O Ref-uge dear, A shel-ter in the time of storm;

Se-cure what-ev-er ill be-tide, A shel-ter in the time of storm.
No fears a-larm, no foes af-fright, A shel-ter in the time of storm.
We'll nev-er leave our safe re-treat, A shel-ter in the time of storm.
Be Thou our help-er ev-er near, A shel-ter in the time of storm.

CHORUS

Oh, Je-sus is a Rock in a wea-ry land, A wea-ry land, a wea-ry land;

Oh, Je-sus is a Rock in a wea-ry land, A shel-ter in the time of storm.

Much Serving

"Eliminate—To thrust out." Did you never hear of the science of elimination? Didn't know there was such a science? Well, just try to eliminate, or to thrust out from your everyday life the unnecessary, hindering things; and if you do not decide that it takes a great deal of knowledge to do so successfully, then I will admit that it was my mistake.

The spring rush is almost upon us [1916]. The little chickens, the garden, the spring sewing and house-cleaning will be on our hands soon, and the worst of it is, they will all come together unless we have been very wise in our planning.

It almost makes one feel like the farmer's wife who called up the stairs to awaken the hired girl on a Monday morning. "Liza Jane," she called, "come hurry and get up and get the breakfast. This is wash day, and here it is almost 6 o'clock and the washing not done yet. Tomorrow is ironing day and the ironing not touched; next day is churning day and it's not begun, and here the week is half gone and nothing done yet."

You'd hardly believe it, but it's true. And it's funny, of course, but one can just feel the worry and strain under which the woman was suffering. All without reason, too, as the greater parts of our worry usually are.

> *Now it came to pass, as they went, that he entered into a certain village: and a certain woman named Martha received him into her house. And she had a sister called Mary, which also sat at Jesus' feet, and heard his word. But Martha was cumbered about much serving, and came to him, and said, Lord, dost thou not care that my sister hath left me to serve alone? bid her therefore that she help me. And Jesus answered and said unto her, Martha, Martha, thou art careful and troubled about many things: but one thing is needful: and Mary hath chosen that good part, which shall not be taken away from her.*
>
> —LUKE 10:38–42

It seems to me that the first thing that should be "thrust out" from our household arrangements is that same worry and feeling of hurry. I do not mean to eliminate haste, for sometimes, usually in fact, that is necessary; but there is a wide difference between haste and hurry. We may make haste with our hands and feet and still keep our minds unhurried. If our minds are cool and collected, our "heads" will be able to "save our heels" a great deal.

An engineer friend once remarked of the housekeeping of a capable woman, "There is no lost motion there." She never worried over her work. She appeared to have no feeling of hurry. Her mind, calm and quiet, directed the work of her hands and there was no bungling, no fruitless running here and there. Every motion and every step counted so that there was "no lost motion."

Household help is so very hard to get, especially on the farm, that with the housekeeper it has become a question of what to leave undone or cut out altogether from her scheme of things as well as how to do in an easier manner what must be done.

The Man of the Place loved good things to eat. Does yet for that matter, as, indeed, I think the men of all other places do. Trying to make him think I was a wonder of a wife, I gratified this appetite until, at last, when planning the dinner for a feast day, I discovered to my horror that there was nothing extra I could cook to mark the day as being distinct and better than any other day. Pies, the best I could make, were common everyday affairs. Cakes, ditto. Puddings, preserves, and jellies were ordinary things. Fried, roasted, broiled, and boiled poultry of all kinds was no treat, we had so much of it as well as other kinds of meat raised on the farm. By canning and pickling and preserving all kinds of vegetables and fruits, we had each and every kind the year around. In fact, we were surfeited with good things to eat all the time.

As I studied the subject, it was impressed upon me that in order to thoroughly enjoy anything, one must feel the absence of it at times, and I acted upon that theory. We have fresh fruit the year around—our apples bridging the gap from blackberries and plums in the summer to the first strawberries in the spring—and these fresh fruits are usually our desserts. Fresh fruits are better, more healthful, more economical, and so much less work to serve than pies, puddings, and preserves. These things we have on our feast days, for Sunday treats, and for company. They are relished so much more because they are something different.

I stopped canning vegetables altogether. There is enough variety in winter vegetables, if rightly used, and we enjoy the green garden truck all the more for having been without it for a few months. The family is just as well if not better satisfied under this treatment, and a great deal of hard work is left out.

Some time ago the semi-annual house-cleaning was dropped from my program, very much to everyone's advantage. If a room needed cleaning out of season, I used to think "Oh well, it will soon be house-cleaning time" and let it wait until then. I found that I was becoming like the man who did "wish Saturday would hurry and come" so that he could take a bath. Then I decided I would have no more house-cleaning in the accepted meaning of that word.

The first step in the new order of things was to dispense with carpets and use rugs instead. When a rug needs shaking and airing, it gets it then, or as soon as possible, instead of waiting until house-cleaning time. If the windows need washing, they are washed the first day I feel energetic enough. The house is gone over in this way a little at a time when it is needed and as suits my convenience, and about all that is left of the bugaboo of house-cleaning is the putting up of the heater in the spring and the taking it out in the fall.

Never do I have the house in a turmoil and myself exhausted as it used to be when I house-cleaned twice a year.

To be sure there are limits to the lessening of work. I could hardly go so far as a friend who said, "Why sweep? If I let it go today and tomorrow and the next day, there will be just so much gained, for the floor will be just as clean when I do sweep, as it would be if I swept every day from now until then." Still, after all, there is something to be said for that viewpoint. The applied science of the elimination of work can best be studied by each housekeeper for herself, but believe me, it is well worth studying.

During the first years of his married life, a man of my acquaintance used to complain bitterly to his wife because she did not make enough slop in the kitchen to keep a hog. "At home," he said, "they always kept a couple of hogs, and they did not cost a cent, for there was always enough waste and slop from the kitchen to feed them." How ridiculous we all are at times! This man actually thought that something was wrong instead of being thankful that there was no waste from his kitchen. The young wife was grieved, but said she did not "like to cook well enough to cook things and throw them to the hogs for the sake of cooking more."

The food on her table was always good, even if some of it was made over dishes; and after a time, her husband realized that he had a treasure in the kitchen, and that it was much cheaper to feed the hogs their proper food than to give them what had been prepared for human consumption.

There are so many little heedless ways in which a few cents are wasted here and a few more there. The total would be truly surprising if we should sum them up. I illustrated this to myself in an odd way lately. While looking over the pages of a catalog advertising articles from two cents to ten cents, the Man of the Place said, "There are a good many little tricks you'd like to have. Get what you want; they will only cost a few cents." So, I made out a list of what I wanted, things I decided I could not get along without as I found them, one by one, on those alluring pages. I was surprised when I added up the cost to find that it amounted to five dollars. I put the list away intending to go over it and cut out some things to make the total less. That was several months ago, and I have not yet missed any of the things I would have ordered. I have decided to let the list wait until I do.

Enjoying the Pilgrim Journey of Life

As I was passing through the Missouri Building, at the exposition last summer [1915], I overheard a scrap of conversation between two women. Said the first woman, "How do you like San Francisco?" The other replied, "I don't like San Francisco at all! Everywhere I go there is a Chinaman on one side, a Jap on the other, and a n——r behind."

These women were missing a great deal, for the foreign life of San Francisco is very interesting; and the strange vari-colored peoples on the streets give a touch of color and picturesqueness that adds much to the charm of the city. A morning's walk from the top of Russian Hill, where I lived when there, would take me through "Little Italy" where one hears Italian spoken on all sides; where the people are black-eyed and handsome with a foreign beauty and where, I am sure, the children are the most beautiful in the world.

> *Boast not thyself of tomorrow; for thou knowest not*
> *what a day may bring forth.*
> —PROVERBS 27:1

From there I passed directly into "Chinatown" where the quaint babies look exactly like Chinese dolls, and the older people look exactly as if they had stepped out of a Chinese picture. The women, in their comfortable loose garments made of black or soft colored silks, with their shiny, smoothly combed black hair full of bright ornaments, were, some of them, very pretty. Only the older men seemed to be wearing the Chinese dress. The younger men were dressed like any American businessman.

It is a curious fact that the second generation of Chinese born in San Francisco are much larger than their parents and look a great deal more like our own people, while the third generation can scarcely be distinguished from Americans. And oh, the shops of Chinatown! I do not understand how any woman could resist their fascination. Such quaint and beautiful jewelry, such wonderful pieces of carved ivory, such fine pottery, and such silks and embroideries as one finds there!

Wandering on from Chinatown, I would soon be at Market Street, which is the main business street of San Francisco; and everywhere, as the women in the Missouri Building had said, there was "a China-man on one side, a Jap on the other, and a n——r behind."

It gives a stay-at-home Middle Westerner something of a shock to meet a group of turbaned Hindoos on the street or a Samoan or a Fil-ipino or even a Mexican. People in happier times spent hundreds of dollars and months of time in traveling to see these foreign people and their manner of living. It is all to be seen, on a smaller scale, in this city of our own country.

Walking on the Zone one day at the fair, Daughter and I noticed ahead of us five sailormen. They were walking along discussing which one of the attractions they should visit. They were evidently on shore for a frolic. Tired of "rocking in the cradle of the deep," they were going to enjoy something different on shore. Should they see the wonderful educated horse? "No! Who cared anything about an old horse?" Should they see Creation, the marvelous electrical display? "No! Not that! We're here for a good time, aren't we?"

Perhaps by now you suspect that Daughter and I had become so interested, we determined to know which of the attractions they decided was worthwhile. We followed with the crowd at their heels. The sailors passed the places of amusement one after another until they came to a mimic river, with a wharf and row boats, oars and all. Immediately, they made a rush for the wharf, and the last we saw of them they were tumbling hilariously into one of the boats for a good old row on the pleasant, familiar water.

Do you know, they reminded me in some way of the women in the Missouri Building who did not like San Francisco.

A friend of mine used to sympathize with a woman for being "tied down" to a farm with no opportunity to travel or to study and with none of the advantages of town or city life. To her surprise she found that her sympathy was not needed. "My body may be tied here," her friend said, "but my mind is free. Books and papers are cheap and what I cannot buy, I can borrow. I have traveled all over the world."

The daughter of this woman was raised with a varied assortment of these same books and papers, pictures and magazines. When later she traveled over the United States, becoming familiar with the larger cities as well as the country, from Canada to the Gulf and from San Francisco to New York City, she said there was a great disappointment to her in traveling. She seemed to have seen it all before and thus had no "thrills" from viewing strange things. "I have read about foreign countries just as much," she said, "and I don't suppose I'll find anything in the world that will be entirely new to me," which shows that a very good travel education can be had from books and papers and also proves once more the old saying that, "As the twig is bent the tree inclines."

Over at a neighbor's the other day, I learned something new as, by the way, quite often happens. She has little soft homemade mattresses as thick as a good comforter to lay over the top of the large mattresses on her beds. Over these small mattresses she slips a cover as one does a case on a pillow. They are easily removed for washing and protect the mattress from soil, making it a simple matter to keep the beds clean and sweet.

This neighbor also makes her sheets last twice as long by a little trick she has. When the sheets begin to wear thin in the middle, she tears them down the center and sews the outsides together. Then she hems the outer edges down the sides. This throws the thin part to the outside and the center, where the wear comes, is as good as new. Of course, the sheet has a seam down the middle, but it is not so very many years ago that all our sheets were that way, before we had sheeting and pillow tubing.

It is no use trying! I seem unable today to get away from the idea of travel, perhaps because I read the *National Geographic* magazine last night. A sentence in one of the articles keeps recurring to me, and I am going to quote it to you, for you may not have noticed it. "It is not a figure of speech to say that every American has it in his heart that he is in a small sense a discoverer; that he is joining in the revelation to the world of something that it was not before aware of and of which it may someday make use."

We have the right, you know, to take a thought and appropriate it to our own uses; and so I have been turning this one over and over in my mind with all sorts of strange ramifications. The greater number of us cannot be discoverers of the kind referred to in the article quoted, for like the woman before mentioned, our bodies are tied more or less securely to our home habitat; but I am sure we are all discoverers at heart.

Life is often called a journey, "the journey of life." Usually when referred to in these terms it is also understood that it is "a weary pilgrimage." Why not call it a voyage of discovery and take it in the spirit of happy adventure?

Adventurers and travelers worthy of the name always make nothing of the difficulties they meet, nor are they so intent on the goal that they do not make discoveries on the way. Has anyone ever said to you, as a warning, "No man knoweth what a day may bring forth?" I have heard it often, and it is always quoted with a melancholy droop at the corners of the mouth. But why! Suppose we do not know what will happen tomorrow. May it not just as well be a happy surprise as something unpleasant?

To me, it is a joy that "no man knoweth what a day may bring forth," and that life is a journey from one discovery to another. It makes of every day a real adventure; and if things are not to my liking today, why, "There's a whole day tomorrow that ain't teched yet," as the old man said. "No man knoweth" what the day will be like. It is absolutely undiscovered country. I'll just travel along and find out for myself.

Did you ever take a little trip anywhere with your conscience easy about things at home, your mind free from worry, and with all care cast aside and eyes wide open give yourself to the joy of every passing incident, looking for interesting things which happen every moment? If you have, you will understand. If not, you should try it, and you will be surprised how much of adventure can enter into ordinary things.

Loving God's Creatures

A redbird swinging in the grape arbor saw himself in the glass of my kitchen window not long ago. He tried to fly thru the glass to reach the strange bird he saw there, and when his little mate came flitting by, he tried to fight his reflection. Apparently, he was jealous. During all one day he fretted and struggled to drive the stranger away. He must have told his little wife about it that night, I think, for in the morning they came to the arbor together, and she alighted before the window while he stayed in the background. She gave Mr. Redbird one look after glancing in the glass, then turned and flew fiercely at her reflection, twittering angrily. One could imagine her saying: "So, that's it! This strange lady Redbird is the reason for your hanging around here instead of getting busy building the nest. I'll soon drive her away!" She tried to fight the strange lady bird until her husband objected to her paying so much attention to her rival; and then they took turns, he declaring there was a gentleman there, she vowing there was a lady and doing her best to drive her away. At last between them, they seemed to understand; and now they both come occasionally to swing on the grapevine before the window and admire themselves in the glass.

There are many interesting things in the out-of-doors life that come so close to us in the country, and if we show a little kindness to the wild creatures, they quickly make friends with us and permit us a delightful intimacy with them and their homes. A bird in a cage is not a pretty sight to me, but it is a pleasure to have the wild birds and the squirrels nesting around the house and so tame that they do not mind our watching them. Persons who shoot or allow shooting on their farms drive away a great deal of amusement and pleasure with the game, as well as do themselves pecuniary damage, while a small boy with a stone handy can do even more mischief than a man with a gun.

> *And God said, Let us make man in our image, after our likeness; and let them have dominion over the fish of the sea, and over the fowl of the air, and over the cattle, and over all the earth, and over every creeping thing that creepeth upon the earth. So God created man in his own image, in the image of God created he him; male and female created he them. And God blessed them, and God said unto them, Be fruitful, and multiply, and replenish the earth, and subdue it: and have dominion over the fish of the sea, and over the fowl of the air, and over every living thing that moveth upon the earth.*
>
> —GENESIS 1:26–28

It is surprising how like human beings animals seem when they are treated with consideration. Did you ever notice the sense of humor animals have? Ever see a dog apologize—not a cringing fawn-ing for favor, but a frank apology as one gentleman to another?

Shep was trying to learn to sit up and shake hands, but try as he would, he could not seem to get the knack of keeping his balance in the upright position. He was an old dog, and you know it has been said that, "It is hard to teach an old dog new tricks." No sympathy has ever been wasted on the dog, but I can assure you that it also is hard for the old dog. After a particularly disheartening session one day, we saw him out on the back porch alone and not knowing that he was observed. He was practicing his lesson without a teacher. We watched while he tried and failed several times, then finally got the trick of it and sat up with his paw extended. The next time we said, "How do you do, Shep?" he had his lesson perfectly. After that it was easy to teach him to fold his paws and be a "Teddy Bear" and to tell us what he said to tramps. We never asked him to lie down and roll over. He was not that kind of character. Shep never would do his tricks for anyone but us, though he would shake hands with others when we told him to do so. His eyesight became poor as he grew older, and he did not always recognize his friends. Once he made a mistake and barked savagely at an old friend whom he really regarded as one of the family, though he had not seen him for some time.

Later, as we all sat in the yard, Shep seemed uneasy. Evidently, there was something on his mind. At last he walked deliberately to the visitor, sat up, and held out his paw. It was so plainly an apology that our friend said: "That's all right, Shep, old fellow! Shake and for-get it!" Shep shook hands and walked away perfectly satisfied.

My little French Poodle, Incubus, is blind. He used to be very active and run about the farm, but his chief duty, as he saw it, was to protect me. Although he cannot see, he still performs that duty, guarding me at night and flying at any stranger who comes too near me during the day. Of what he is thinking when he sits for long periods in the yard with his face to the sun, I am too stupid to understand perfectly, but I feel that in his little doggy heart, he is asking the eternal "Why?" as we all do at times. After a while he seemingly decides to make the best of it and takes a walk around the familiar places or comes in the house and does his little tricks for candy with a cheery good will.

If patience and cheerfulness and courage, if being faithful to our trust and doing our duty under difficulties count for so much in man that he expects to be rewarded for them, both here and hereafter, how are they any less in the life of my little blind dog? Surely, such virtues in animals are worth counting in the sum total of good in the universe.

How to Furnish a Home

As someone has said, "Thoughts are things," and the atmosphere of every home depends on the kind of thoughts each member of that home is thinking.

I spent an afternoon a short time ago with a friend in her new home. The house was beautiful and well-furnished with new furniture, but it seemed bare and empty to me. I wondered why this was until I remembered my experience with my new house. I could not make the living room seem homelike. I would move the chairs here and there and change the pictures on the wall, but something was lacking. Nothing seemed to change the feeling of coldness and vacancy that displeased me whenever I entered the room.

Then, as I stood in the middle of the room one day wondering what I could possibly do to improve it, it came to me that all that was needed was for someone to live in it and furnish it with the everyday, pleasant thoughts of friendship and cheerfulness and hospitality.

We all know there is a spirit in every home, a sort of composite spirit composed of the thoughts and feelings of the members of the family as a composite photograph is formed of the features of different individuals. This spirit meets us at the door as we enter the home. Sometimes it is a friendly, hospitable spirit, and sometimes it is cold and forbidding.

> *Better is a little with the fear of the LORD than great treasure and trouble therewith. Better is a dinner of herbs where love is, than a stalled ox and hatred therewith. A wrathful man stirreth up strife: but he that is slow to anger appeaseth strife.*
> —PROVERBS 15:16–18

If the members of a home are ill-tempered and quarrelsome, how quickly you feel it when you enter the house. You may not know just what is wrong, but you wish to make your visit short. If they are kindly, generous, good-tempered people, you will have a feeling of warmth and welcome that will make you wish to stay. Sometimes you feel that you must be very prim and dignified, and at another place you feel a rollicking good humor and a readiness to laugh and be merry. Poverty or riches, old style housekeeping or modern conveniences do not affect your feelings. It is the characters and personalities of the persons who live there.

Each individual has a share in making this atmosphere of the home what it is, but the mother can mold it more to her wishes.

> *It is better to dwell in the wilderness, than with a contentious and an angry woman.*
> —PROVERBS 21:19

I read a piece of poetry several years ago that was supposed to be a man speaking of his wife, and this was the refrain of the little story:

> I love my wife because she laughs,
> Because she laughs and doesn't care.

I'm sure that would have been a delightful home to visit, for a good laugh overcomes more difficulties and dissipates more dark clouds than any other one thing. And this woman was the embodied spirit of cheerfulness and good temper.

Let's be cheerful! We have no more right to steal the brightness out of the day for our own family than we have to steal the purse of a stranger. Let us be as careful that our homes are furnished with pleasant and happy thoughts as we are that the rugs are the right color and texture and the furniture comfortable and beautiful!

The Blessings of the Year

Among all the blessings of the year, have you chosen one for which to be especially thankful at this Thanksgiving time or are you unable to decide which is the greatest?

Sometimes we recognize as a special blessing what heretofore we have taken without a thought as a matter of course, as when we recover from a serious illness; just a breath drawn free from pain is a matter for rejoicing. If we have been crippled and then are whole again, the blessed privilege of walking forth free and unhindered seems a gift from the "gods." We must have been hungry to properly appreciate food, and we never love our friends as we should until they have been taken from us.

> *Giving thanks always for all things unto God and the*
> *Father in the name of our Lord Jesus Christ; submit-*
> *ting yourselves one to another in the fear of God.*
> —EPHESIANS 5:20

As the years pass, I am coming more and more to understand that it is the common, everyday blessings of our common everyday lives for which we should be particularly grateful. They are the things that fill our lives with comfort and our hearts with gladness—just the pure air to breathe and the strength to breathe it; just warmth and shelter and home folks; just plain food that gives us strength; the bright sunshine on a cold day; and a cool breeze when the day is warm.

Oh, we have so much to be thankful for that we seldom think of it in that way! I wish we might think more about these things that we are so much inclined to overlook and live more in the spirit of the old Scotch table blessing.

Some hae meat wha canna' eat
And some can eat that lack it.
But I hae meat and I can eat
And sae the Laird be thankit.

Not So Bad Off

My community is representative of those rural districts which come in for much solicitude because of their backward state. Our children are among those pitied because of their lack of a chance equal to the negro in the cities for a proper start in life [1922]. I used to be mortally sick because I believed this. Today I doubt it.

A chance is not everything. Besides:

In our schoolhouse, where stoves are still unjacketed, the children meet one day out of seven to receive religious training.

In the city, where children are supposed to have everything, thousands are growing up without the most important part of an education—proper home training.

We country mothers, realizing the dearth of so-called advantages, strive that at least home and neighborhood influences shall be of the best.

> *Better it is to be of an humble spirit with the lowly, than to divide the spoil with the proud. He that handleth a matter wisely shall find good: and whoso trusteth in the LORD, happy is he. The wise in heart shall be called prudent: and the sweetness of the lips increaseth learning.*
>
> —PROVERBS 16:19–21

Because it takes us all to make a go of any cooperative work or pastime, we learn to work harmoniously together. This is good for the children to see.

We read good books. We have our community sings. Also, we have prayer meetings where young mothers pray and where boys and girls get up and say: "Lord, that I may be a little kinder, a little braver to meet temptation, a little more thoughtful of my neighbor."

The object of all education is to make folks fit to live. I guess we are not so bad off.

Would You Rather Have Times or Things?

My neighbor, who came from a city where her husband worked for a salary, said to me, "It is difficult for anyone who has worked for wages to get used to farming. There is a great difference between having a good paycheck coming twice a month or having only the little cash one can take in on a small farm. Why we have scarcely any money at all to spend!"

"You spent the paycheck for your living expenses, did you not?" I asked.

"All of it," she answered. "Every bit! We never could save a cent of it."

"And you have your living now, off the farm," said I.

"Yes, and a good one," she replied, "with a little left over. But it was great fun spending the paycheck. If we'd had a little less fun, we might have had more left."

All of which brings us to the question the little girl asked: "Would you rather have times or things"—good times to remember or things to keep, like bank accounts, homes of our own, and such things?

> *To every thing there is a season, and a time to every purpose under the heaven: a time to be born, and a time to die; a time to plant, and a time to pluck up that which is planted; a time to kill, and a time to heal; a time to break down, and a time to build up; a time to weep, and a time to laugh; a time to mourn, and a time to dance; a time to cast away stones, and a time to gather stones together; a time to embrace, and a time to refrain from embracing; a time to get, and a time to lose; a time to keep, and a time to cast away; a time to rend, and a time to sew; a time to keep silence, and a time to speak; a time to love, and a time to hate; a time of war, and a time of peace. What profit hath he that worketh in that wherein he laboureth? I have seen the travail, which God hath given to the sons of men to be exercised in it. He hath made every thing beautiful in his time: also he hath set the world in their heart, so that no man can find out the work that God maketh from the beginning to the end. I know that there is no good in them, but for a man to rejoice, and to do good in his life. And also that every man should eat and drink, and enjoy the good of all his labour, it is the gift of God.*
> —ECCLESIASTES 3:1–13

Things alone are very unsatisfying. Happiness is not to be found in money or in houses and lands, not even in modern kitchens or a late model motor car. Such things add to our happiness only because of the pleasant times they bring us.

But times would be bad without some things. We cannot enjoy ourselves if we are worried over how we shall pay our bills or the taxes or buy what the children need. And so we must mix our times and things, but let's mix 'em with brains, as the famous artist said he mixed his paints, using good judgment in the amount we take.

With All Thy Getting, Get Understanding

Mrs. Brown was queer. The neighbors all thought so, and, what was worse, they said so.

Mrs. Fuller happened in several times, quite early in the morning, and although the work was not done up, Mrs. Brown was sitting leisurely in her room or else she would be writing at her desk. Then Mrs. Powers went through the house one afternoon, and the dishes were stacked back unwashed, the bed still airing, and everything "at sixes and sevens," except the room where Mrs. Brown seemed to be idling away her time. Mrs. Powers said Mrs. Brown was "just plain lazy," and she didn't care who heard her say it.

Ida Brown added interesting information when she told her schoolmates, after school, that she must hurry home and do up the work. It was a shame, the neighbors said, that Mrs. Brown should idle away her time all day and leave the work for Ida to do after school.

Later, it was learned that Mrs. Brown had been writing for the papers to earn money to buy Ida's new winter outfit. Ida had been glad to help by doing the work after school so that her mother might have the day for study and writing, but they had not thought it necessary to explain to the neighbors.

> *Judge not, that ye be not judged. For with what judgment ye judge, ye shall be judged: and with what measure ye mete, it shall be measured to you again. And why beholdest thou the mote that is in thy brother's eye, but considerest not the beam that is in thine own eye? Or how wilt thou say to thy brother, Let me pull out the mote out of thine eye; and, behold, a beam is in thine own eye? Thou hypocrite, first cast out the beam out of thine own eye; and then shalt thou see clearly to cast out the mote out of thy brother's eye.*
>
> —MATTHEW 7:1–5

I read a little verse a few years ago entitled, "If We Only Understood," and the refrain was, "We would love each other better, If we only understood."

I have forgotten the author and last verse, but the refrain has remained in my memory and comes to my mind every now and then when I hear unkind remarks made about people.

The things that people do would look so differently to us if we only understood the reasons for their actions, nor would we blame them so much for their faults if we knew all the circumstances of their lives. Even their sins might not look so hideous if we could feel what pressure and perhaps suffering had caused them.

The safest course is to be as understanding as possible, and, where our understanding fails, to call charity to its aid. Learn to distinguish between persons and the things they do, and while we may not always approve of their actions, have a sympathy and feeling of kindness for the persons themselves.

It may even be that what we consider faults and weaknesses in others are only prejudices on our own part. Some of us would like to see everybody fitted to our own pattern, and what a tiresome world this would be if that were done. We should be willing to allow others the freedom we demand for ourselves. Everyone has the right to self-expression.

If we keep this genial attitude toward the world and the people in it, we will keep our own minds and feelings healthy and clean. Even the vigilance necessary to guard our thoughts in this way will bring us rewards in better disciplined minds and happier dispositions.

204 **Happy Land.**

Old Melody.

1. There is a hap-py land, Far, far a-way, Where saints in glo - ry stand,
2. Bright, in that hap-py land, Beams ev - 'ry eye; Kept by a Father's hand,
3. Come to that hap-py land, Come, come a-way; Why will you doubting stand?

Bright, bright as day; Oh, how they sweet-ly sing, "Wor-thy is our
Love can-not die. Oh, then, to glo - ry run; Be a crown and
Why still de - lay? Oh, we shall hap-py be, When from sin and

Sav - ior King;" Loud let His prais - es ring, Praise, praise for aye!
king-dom won; And bright, a - bove the sun, Reign ev - er-more.
sor - row free, Lord, we shall dwell with Thee, Blest ev - er-more.

The Armor of a Smile

Mrs. A was angry. Her eyes snapped, her voice was shrill, and a red flag of rage was flying upon each cheek. She expected opposition and anger at the things she said, but her remarks were answered in a soft voice; her angry eyes were met by smiling ones; and her attack was smothered in the softness of courtesy, consideration, and compromise.

I feel sure Mrs. A had intended to create a disturbance, but she might as well have tried to break a feather pillow by beating it as to have any effect with her angry voice and manner on the perfect kindness and good manners which met her. She only made herself ridiculous, and in self-defense was obliged to change her attitude.

Since then I have been wondering if it always is so, if shafts of malice aimed in anger forever fall harmless against the armor of a smile, kind words, and gentle manners. I believe they do. And I have gained a fuller understanding of the words, "A soft answer turneth away wrath" (Prov. 15:1).

> *But now ye also put off all these; anger, wrath, malice, blasphemy, filthy communication out of your mouth. . . . Put on therefore, as the elect of God, holy and beloved, bowels of mercies, kindness, humbleness of mind, meekness, longsuffering; forbearing one another, and forgiving one another, if any man have a quarrel against any: even as Christ forgave you, so also do ye.*
> —COLOSSIANS 3:8; 12–13

Until this incident, I had found no more in the words than the idea that a soft answer might cool the wrath of an aggressor, but I saw wrath turned away as an arrow deflected from its mark and came to understand that a soft answer and a courteous manner are an actual protection.

Nothing is ever gained by allowing anger to have sway. While under its influence, we lose the ability to think clearly and lose the forceful power that is in calmness.

Anger is a destructive force; its purpose is to hurt and destroy, and being a blind passion, it does its evil work, not only upon whatever arouses it, but also upon the person who harbors it. Even physically it injures him, impeding the action of the heart and circulation, affecting the respiration, and creating an actual poison in the blood. Persons with weak hearts have been known to drop dead from it, and always there is a feeling of illness after indulging in a fit of temper.

Anger is a destroying force. What all the world needs is its opposite—an uplifting power.

The Value of Good Words

The snow was falling fast and a cold wind blowing the other morning. I had just come in from feeding the chickens and was warming my chilled self when the telephone rang.

"Hello!" said I, and a voice full of laughter came over a wire.

"Good morning!" it said. "I suppose you are busy making garden today."

"Making garden?" I asked wonderingly.

"Yes," replied the voice, "you said some time ago that you enjoyed making garden in the wintertime beside a good fire, so I thought you'd be busily at it this morning."

"Well," I replied defensively, "the vegetables one raises in the seed catalogs are so perfectly beautiful." And with a good laugh, we began the day right merrily in spite of the storm outside.

A merry heart maketh a cheerful countenance: but by sorrow of the heart the spirit is broken.
—PROVERBS 15:13

So after many days my words came back to me and the thoughts that followed them were altogether different from those connected with them before.

We do grow beautiful gardens beside the fire on cold winter days as we talk over the seed catalogs; and our summer gardens are much more of a success because of these gardens in our minds. We grow many other things in the same way. It is truly surprising how anything grows and grows by talking about it.

We have a slight headache and we mention the fact. As an excuse to ourselves for inflicting it upon our friends, we make it as bad as possible in the telling. "Oh, I have such a dreadful headache," we say and immediately we feel much worse. Our pain has grown by talking of it.

A wholesome tongue is a tree of life: but perverseness therein is a breach in the spirit.
—PROVERBS 15:4

If there is a disagreement between friends and the neighbors begin talking about it, the difficulty grows like a jimson weed, and the more it is talked about the faster it grows.

When there is a disagreement between workmen and their employers, the agitators immediately begin their work of talking and the trouble grows and grows until strikes and lockouts and riots are ripened and harvested and the agitators grow fat on the fruits thereof.

The same law seems to work in both human nature and in the vegetable kingdom and in the world of ideas with the changes caused just by talk, either positive or negative. Even peas and cabbages grow by cultivation, by keeping the soil "stirred" about them.

Now it isn't enough in any garden to cut down the weeds. The cutting out of weeds is important, but cultivating the garden plants is just as necessary. If we want vegetables, we must make them grow, not leave the ground barren where we have destroyed the weeds. Just so we must give much of our attention to the improvements we want, not all to the abuses we would like to correct. If we hope to improve conditions, any conditions, anywhere, we must do a great deal of talking about the better things.

If we have a headache we will forget it sooner if we talk of pleasant things. If there is misunderstanding and bad feeling between neighbors, we can cultivate their friendliness by telling each of the other's kind words before the trouble began. Perhaps a crust has formed around the plant of their friendship, and it only needs that the soil should be stirred in order to keep on growing.

Remember the Sabbath

The whole world was a deep, dark blue, for I had waked with a grouch that morning. While blue is without doubt a heavenly color, it is better in skies than in one's mind; for when the blues descend upon a poor mortal on earth, life seems far from being worth the living.

I didn't want to help with the chores; I hated to get breakfast; and the prospect of doing up the morning's work afterward was positively revolting. Beginning the usual round of duties—under protest—I had a great many thoughts about work and none of them was complimentary to the habit. But presently my mind took a wider range and became less personal as applied to the day just beginning.

First, I remembered the old, old labor law: "Six days shalt thou labour, and do all thy work: but the seventh day is the sabbath of the Lord thy God: in it thou shalt not do any work" (Exod. 20:9–10).

It used to be impressed upon us as most important that we must rest on the seventh day. This doesn't seem to be necessary any longer. We may not "Remember the sabbath day, to keep it holy" (Exod. 20:8), but we'll not forget to stop working. With our present attitude toward work, the emphasis should be put upon "Six days thou shalt labor," and if we stick it out to work the six days, we will rest on the seventh without any urging.

Given half a chance, we will take Saturday off also and any other day or part of a day we can manage to sneak, besides which the length of a work day is shrinking and shrinking for everyone except farmers, and they are hoping to shorten theirs.

> *In all labour there is profit: but the talk of the lips tendeth only to penury.*
>
> —PROVERBS 14:23

But really the old way was best, for it takes about six days of work to give just the right flavor to a day off. As I thought of all these things, insensibly, my ideas about work changed. I remembered the time of enforced idleness when recovering from an illness and how I longed to be busily at work again. Also I recollected a week of vacation that I once devoted to pleasure during which I suffered more than the weariness of working while I had none of its satisfaction. For there is a great satisfaction in work well done, the thrill of success in a task accomplished.

I got the thrill at the moment that my mind reached the climax. The separator was washed. It is a job that I especially dislike, but while my mind had been busy far afield, my hands had performed their accustomed task with none of the usual sense of unpleasantness, showing that, after all, it is not so much the work we do with our bodies that makes us tired and dissatisfied as the work we do with our minds.

We have been, for so long, thinking of labor as a curse upon man that, because of our persistently thinking of it as such, it has very nearly become so.

There always has been a great deal of misplaced pity for Adam because of his sentence to hard labor for life when really that was all that saved him after he was deported from paradise, and it is the only thing that has kept his descendants as safe and sane even as they are.

> *Go to the ant, thou sluggard; consider her ways, and be wise: which having no guide, overseer, or ruler, provideth her meat in the summer, and gathereth her food in the harvest. How long wilt thou sleep, O sluggard? when wilt thou arise out of thy sleep? Yet a little sleep, a little slumber, a little folding of the hands to sleep: so shall thy poverty come as one that travelleth, and thy want as an armed man.*
>
> —PROVERBS 6:6–11

There is nothing wrong with God's plan that man should earn his bread by the sweat of his brow. The wrong is in our own position only. In trying to shirk while we "let George do it," we bring upon ourselves our own punishment; for in the attitude we take toward our work, we make of it a burden instead of the blessing it might be.

Work is like other good things in that it should not be indulged in to excess, but a reasonable amount that is of value to one's self and to the world, as is any honest, well-directed labor, need never descend into drudgery.

It is a tonic and an inspiration and a reward unto itself. For the sweetness of life lies in usefulness like honey deep in the heart of a clover bloom.

A Time for Reflection

There is a purple haze over the hilltops and a hint of sadness in the sunshine because of summer's departure; on the low ground down by the spring the walnuts are dropping from the trees and squirrels are busy hiding away their winter supply. Here and there the leaves are beginning to change color and a little vagrant autumn breeze goes wandering over the hills and down the valleys whispering to "follow, follow," until it is almost impossible to resist. So I should not be too harshly criticized if I ramble a little even in my conversation.

We have been gathering the fruits of the season's work into barns and bins and cellars. The harvest has been abundant, and a good supply is stored away for future needs.

Now I am wondering what sort of fruits and how plentiful is the supply we have stored away in our hearts and souls and minds from our year's activities. The time of gathering together the visible results of our year's labor is a very appropriate time to reckon up the invisible, more important harvest.

When we lived in South Dakota where the cold came early and strong, we once had a hired man (farmers had them in those days), who was a good worker, but whose money was too easily spent. In the fall when the first cold wind struck him, he would shiver and chatter and, always he would say, "Gee Mighty! This makes a feller wonder what's become of his summer's wages!"

> LORD, *make me to know mine end, and the measure of*
> *my days, what it is; that I may know how frail I am.*
> *Behold, thou hast made my days as an handbreadth;*
> *and mine age is as nothing before thee: verily every*
> *man at his best state is altogether vanity.*
>
> —PSALM 39:4–5

Ever since then, Harvest Home time has seemed to me the time to gather together and take stock of our mental and spiritual harvest, and to wonder what we have done with the wealth of opportunity that has come to us, and the treasures we have had in our keeping. Much too often I have felt like quoting the hired man of other days.

Have we found a new friendship worthwhile? Have we even kept safely the old friendships, treasures worth much more than silver and gold? People in these history-making days hold their opinions so strongly and defend them so fiercely that a strain will be put upon many friendships; and the pity of it is that these misunderstandings will come between people who are earnestly striving for the right thing. Right seems to be obscured and truth is difficult to find.

But if the difficulty of finding the truth has increased our appreciation of its value, if the beauty of truth is plainer to us and more desired, then we have gathered treasure for the future.

*Blessed is the man that walketh not in the counsel of
the ungodly, nor standeth in the way of sinners, nor
sitteth in the seat of the scornful. But his delight is in
the law of the LORD; and in his law doth he meditate
day and night. And he shall be like a tree planted by
the rivers of water, that bringeth forth his fruit in his
season; his leaf also shall not wither; and whatsoever
he doeth shall prosper.*

—PSALM 1:1–3

We lay away the gleanings of our years in the edifice of our character where nothing is ever lost. What have we stored away in this safe place during the season that is past? Is it something that will keep sound and pure and sweet or something that is faulty and not worth storing?

As a child I learned my Bible lessons by heart in the good old-fashioned way, and once won the prize for repeating correctly more verses from the Bible than any other person in the Sunday school. But always my mind had a trick of picking a text here and a text there and connecting them together in meaning. In this way there came to me a thought that makes the stores from my invisible harvest important to me. These texts are familiar to everyone. It is their sequence that gives the thought.

"Lay not up for yourselves treasures upon earth, where moth and rust doth corrupt, and where thieves break through and steal: but lay up for yourselves treasures in heaven, where neither moth nor rust doth corrupt, and where thieves do not break through nor steal" (Matt. 6:19–20).

And then: "Neither shall they say, Lo here! or, lo there! for, behold, the kingdom of God is within you" (Luke 17:21).

Jerusalem, the Golden

EWING. 7. 6. 7. 6. D.

BERNARD OF CLUNY, 12th Century
Tr. by JOHN M. NEALE, 1818-1866

ALEXANDER EWING, 1830-1895

1. Je - ru - sa - lem, the gold - en, With milk and hon - ey blest!
2. They stand, those halls of Zi - on, All ju - bi - lant with song,
3. O sweet and bless - ed Coun - try, Shall I e'er see thy face?

Be - neath thy con - tem - pla - tion Sink heart and voice op-pressed;
And bright with man - y an an - gel, And all the mar - tyr throng;
O sweet and bless - ed Coun - try, Shall I e'er win thy grace?

I know not, O I know not What joys a - wait me there;
The Prince is ev - er in them, The day - light is se - rene;
Ex - ult, O dust and ash - es! The Lord shall be thy part;

What ra - dian - cy of glo - ry, What bliss be-yond com-pare.
The pas - tures of the bless - ed Are decked in glo - rious sheen.
His on - ly, His for - ev - er, Thou shalt be, and thou art! A - MEN.

Thanks for the Harvest

The season is over [1921], the rush and struggle of growing and saving the crops is past for another year, and the time has come when we pause and reverently give thanks for the harvest. For it is not to our efforts alone that our measure of success is due, but to the life principle in the earth and the seed, to the sunshine and to the rain—to the goodness of God.

We may not be altogether satisfied with the year's results, and we can do a terrific amount of grumbling when we take the notion. But I am sure we all know in our hearts that we have a great deal for which to be thankful. In spite of disappointment and weariness and perhaps sorrow, His goodness and mercy does follow us all the days of our lives.

> *This I recall to my mind, therefore have I hope. It is of the LORD's mercies that we are not consumed, because his compassions fail not. They are new every morning: great is thy faithfulness. The LORD is my portion, saith my soul; therefore will I hope in him. The LORD is good unto them that wait for him, to the soul that seeketh him. It is good that a man should both hope and quietly wait for the salvation of the LORD.*
> —LAMENTATIONS 3:21–26

As the time approaches when we shall be called upon by proclamation to give thanks, we must decide whether we shall show our thankfulness only by overeating at the Thanksgiving feast. That would seem a rather curious way to show gratitude—simply to grasp greedily what is given!

When a neighbor does us a favor, we show our appreciation of it by doing him a favor in return. Then when the Lord showers favors upon us, how much more should we try to show our gratitude in such ways acceptable to Him, remembering always the words of Christ, "Inasmuch as ye have done it unto one of the least of these my brethren, ye have done it unto me" (Matt. 25:40).

Growing Older with Faith

With the coming of another new year we are all . . . a year older. Just what does it mean to us—this growing older? Are we coming to a cheerful, beautiful old age, or are we being beaten and cowed by the years as they pass?

Bruised we must be now and then, but beaten, never, unless we lack courage.

Not long since a friend said to me, "Growing old is the saddest thing in the world." Since then I have been thinking about growing old, trying to decide if I thought her right. But I cannot agree with her. True, we lose some things that we prize as time passes and acquire a few that we would prefer to be without. But we may gain infinitely more with the years than we lose in wisdom, character, and the sweetness of life.

As to the ills of old age, it may be that those of the past were as bad but are dimmed by the distance. Though old age has gray hair and twinges of rheumatism, remember that childhood has freckles, tonsils, and the measles.

The stream of passing years is like a river with people being carried along in the current. Some are swept along, protesting, fighting all the way, trying to swim back up the stream, longing for the shores that they have passed, clutching at anything to retard their progress, frightened by the onward rush of the strong current and in danger of being overwhelmed by the waters.

Others go with the current freely, trusting themselves to the buoyancy of the waters, knowing they will bear them up. And so with very little effort, they go floating safely along, gaining more courage and strength from their experience with the waves.

> *Trust in the LORD with all thine heart; and lean not unto thine own understanding. In all thy ways acknowledge him, and he shall direct thy paths. Be not wise in thine own eyes: fear the LORD, and depart from evil. It shall be health to thy navel, and marrow to thy bones. Honour the LORD with thy substance, and with the first fruits of all thine increase: so shall thy barns be filled with plenty, and thy presses shall burst out with new wine.*
>
> —PROVERBS 3:5–10

As New Year after New Year comes, these waves upon the river of life bear us farther along toward the ocean of Eternity, either protesting the inevitable and looking longingly back toward years that are gone or with calmness and faith facing the future serene in the knowledge that the power behind life's currents is strong and good.

And thinking of these things, I have concluded that whether it is sad to grow old depends on how we face it, whether we are looking forward with confidence or backward with regret. Still, in any case, it takes courage to live long successfully, and they are brave who grow old with smiling faces.

Treating People Right

"It is always best to treat people right," remarked my lawyer friend.

"Yes, I suppose so in the end," I replied inanely.

"Oh, of course!" he returned, "but that was not what I meant. It pays every time to do the right thing! It pays now and in dollars and cents."

"For instance?" I asked.

"Well, for the latest instance: a man came to me the other day to bring suit against a neighbor. He had good grounds for damages and could win the suit, but it would cost him more than he could recover. It would increase his neighbor's expenses and increase the bad feeling between them. I needed that attorney's fee; but it would not have been doing the right thing to encourage him to bring suit, so I advised him to settle out of court. He insisted, but I refused to take the case. He hired another lawyer, won his case, and paid the difference between the damages he recovered and his expenses."

> *He that walketh righteously, and speaketh uprightly;*
> *he that despiseth the gain of oppressions, that shaketh*
> *his hands from holding of bribes, that stoppeth his ears*
> *from hearing of blood, and shutteth his eyes from see-*
> *ing evil; he shall dwell on high: his place of defence*
> *shall be the munitions of rocks: bread shall be given*
> *him; his waters shall be sure.*
>
> —ISAIAH 33:15–16

"A client came to me a short time afterward with a worthwhile suit and a good retainer's fee, which I could take without robbing him. He was sent to me by the man whose case I had refused to take and because of that very refusal."

Is it possible that "honesty is the best policy," after all, actually and literally? I would take the advice of my lawyer friend on any other business, and I have his word for it that it pays to do the right thing here and now.

To do the right thing is simply to be honest, for being honest is more than refraining from shortchanging a customer or robbing a neighbor's hen roost. To be sure, those items are included, but there is more to honesty than that. There is such a thing as being dishonest when no question of financial gain or loss is involved. When one person robs another of his good name, he is dishonest. When by an unnecessary, unkind act or cross word, one causes another to lose a day or an hour of happiness, is that one not a thief? Many a person robs another of the joy of life while taking pride in his own integrity.

We steal from today to give to tomorrow; we "rob Peter to pay Paul." We are not honest even with ourselves; we rob ourselves of health; we cheat ourselves with sophistries; we even "put an enemy in our mouths to steal away our brains."

If there were a cry of "Stop thief!" we would all stand still. Yet nevertheless in spite of our carelessness, we all know deep in our hearts that it pays to do the right thing, though it is easy to deceive ourselves for a time. If we do the wrong thing, we are quite likely never to know what we have lost by it. If the lawyer had taken the first case, he might have thought he gained by so doing, for he never would have known of the larger fee which came to him by taking the other course.

To Sweep a Room
As to God's Laws

The Man of the Place and I were sitting cozily by the fire. The evening lamp was lighted and the day's papers and the late magazines were scattered over the table. But though we each held in our hands our favorite publications, we were not reading. We were grumbling about the work we had to do and saying all the things usually said at such times.

"People used to have time to live and enjoy themselves, but there is no time anymore for anything but work, work, work."

Oh, we threshed it all over as everyone does when they get that kind of grouch, and then we sat in silence. I was wishing I had lived altogether in those good old days when people had time for things they wanted to do.

What the Man of the Place was thinking, I do not know; but I was quite surprised at the point at which he had arrived, when he remarked out of the silence, in rather a meek voice, "I never realized how much work my father did. Why, one winter he sorted five hundred bushels of potatoes after supper by lantern light. He sold them for $1.50 a bushel in the spring, too, but he must have got blamed tired of sorting potatoes down cellar every night until he had handled more than five hundred bushels of them."

"What did your mother do while your father was sorting potatoes?" I asked.

"Oh, she sewed and knit," said the Man of the Place. "She made all our clothes, coats and pants, undergarments for father and us boys as well as everything she and the girls wore, and she knit all our socks and mittens—shag mittens for the men folks, do you remember, all fuzzy on the outside? She didn't have time enough in the day to do all the work and so she sewed and knit at night."

I looked down at the magazine in my hand and remembered how my mother was always sewing or knitting by the evening lamp. I realized that I never had done so except now and then in cases of emergency.

But the Man of the Place was still talking. "Mother did all her sewing by hand then," he said, "and she spun her own yarn and wove her own cloth. Father harvested his grain by hand with a sickle and cut his hay with a scythe. I do wonder how he ever got it done."

Again we were silent, each busy with our own thoughts. I was counting up the time I give to club work and lodge work and—yes, I'll admit it—politics. My mother and my mother-in-law had none of these, and they do use up a good many hours. Instead of all this, they took time once in a while from their day and night working to go visit a neighbor for the day.

"Time to enjoy life!" Well, they did enjoy it, but it couldn't have been because they had more time.

But let all those that put their trust in thee rejoice: let them ever shout for joy, because thou defendest them: let them also that love thy name be joyful in thee. For thou, LORD, wilt bless the righteous; with favour wilt thou compass him as with a shield.

—PSALM 5:11–12

Why should we need extra time in which to enjoy ourselves? If we expect to enjoy our life, we will have to learn to be joyful in all of it, not just at stated intervals when we can get time or when we have nothing else to do.

It may well be that it is not our work that is so hard for us as the dread of it and our often expressed hatred of it. Perhaps it is our spirit and attitude toward life, and its conditions that are giving us trouble instead of a shortage of time. Surely the days and nights are as long as they ever were.

A feeling of pleasure in a task seems to shorten it wonderfully, and it makes a great difference with the day's work if we get enjoyment from it instead of looking for all our pleasure altogether apart from it, as seems to be the habit of mind we are more and more growing into.

We find in the goods we buy, from farm implements to clothing, that the work of making them is carelessly and slightingly done. Many carpenters, blacksmiths, shoemakers, garment makers, and farm hands do not care how their work is done just so quitting time and the paycheck comes. Farmers are not different except that they must give more attention to how a thing is done because it is the result only that brings them any return.

It seems that many workmen take no pride or pleasure in their work. It is perhaps partly a result of machine-made goods, but it would be much better for us all if we could be more interested in the work of our hands, if we could get back more of the attitude of our mothers toward their handmade garments and of our fathers' pride in their own workmanship. There is an old maxim which I have not heard for years nor thought of in a long time. "To sweep a room as to God's laws, makes that, and the action fine." We need more of that spirit toward our work.

*And whatsoever ye do, do it heartily, as to the Lord,
and not unto men; knowing that of the Lord ye shall
receive the reward of the inheritance: for ye serve the
Lord Christ.*

—Colossians 3:23–24

As I thought of my neighbors and myself, it seemed to me that we were all slighting our work to get time for a joyride of one kind or another.

Not that I object to joyriding! The more the merrier, but I'm hoping for a change of mind that will carry the joy into the work as well as the play.

"All work and no play makes Jack a dull boy," surely, and it makes Jill also very dull indeed; but all play and no work would make hoboes of us. So let's enjoy the work we must do to be respectable.

The Man of the Place had evidently kept right on thinking of the work his father used to do. "Oh, well," he said as he rose and lighted the lantern preparatory to making his late round to see that everything was all right at the barns, "I guess we're not having such a hard time after all. It depends a good deal on how you look at it."

"Yes," said I, "Oh yes, indeed! It depends a good deal on how you look at it."

Personal and National Responsibility: Doing What Is Right

Germany [June 1919, after WW 1] is finding that as a nation that has for four years deliberately broken its pledged word, that word is of no value; that it is bankrupt in moral guarantees.

The entente [Britain and France as allied against Germany] is in the position with Germany of the hill man who fought another man for telling an untruth about him. He had knocked his enemy down and was still beating him though he was crying "enough" when a stranger came along and interfered.

"Stop! Stop!" he exclaimed. "Don't you hear him hollering 'enough'?"

"Oh, yes!" replied the hill man, "but he is such a liar I don't know whether he is telling the truth or not."

When I was a girl at home, my father came in from the harvest field one day at noon and with great glee told what had befallen my cousin Charley. Father and Uncle Henry were harvesting a field of wheat in the old-fashioned way, cutting it by hand with cradles, and Charley, who was about ten years old, followed them around the field for play. He lagged behind until the men where ahead of him and then began to scream, jumping up and down and throwing his arms around. Father and Uncle Henry dropped their cradles and ran to him thinking a snake had bitten him or that something in the woods close by was frightening him; but when they came to Charley, he stopped screaming and laughed at them.

Charley fooled them this way three times, but they grew tired and warm and had been deceived so many times that when, for the fourth time, he began to scream, they looked back at him as he jumped up and down, then turned away and went on with their work.

But Charley kept on screaming, and there seemed to be a new note in his voice, so finally they walked back to where he was and found that he was in a yellow jackets' nest; and the more he jumped and threw and screamed the more came to sting him.

"I'd like to have the training of that young man for a little while," said father, "but I don't believe I could have thought of a better way to punish him for his meanness."

Boys or men or nations, it seems to be the same, if they prove themselves liars times enough, nobody will believe them when they do tell the truth.

> *Let all the earth fear the LORD: let all the inhabitants of the world stand in awe of him. For he spake, and it was done; he commanded, and it stood fast. The LORD bringeth the counsel of the heathen to nought: he maketh the devices of the people of none effect. The counsel of the LORD standeth for ever, the thoughts of his heart to all generations. Blessed is the nation whose God is the LORD; and the people whom he hath chosen for his own inheritance.*
>
> —PSALM 33:8–12

"Getting down to first causes, what makes one nation choose the high way and another nation choose the low way? What produces character and conscience in a nation anyhow? What produces the other thing?" asks a writer in an article in the *Saturday Evening Post*. And the question is left unanswered.

In a country ruled as Germany has been, there is no doubt the character of the nation received the impress of the rulers, coming from them down to the people. In a country such as ours, the national character is also like that of the rulers; but in this case the rulers are the people, and it is they who impress themselves upon it. The character of each individual one of us affects our national character for good or bad.

Getting down to first causes, what forms the character of individuals?

Training! School training; home training; mother's training! And there you are back to the first causes in the making of an honorable, truthful, upright individual, the kind of citizen who collectively makes an honorable, truthful, upright individual, the kind of citizen who collectively makes an honorable, treaty-keeping nation, a nation that chooses the high way instead of the low.

My Country, 'Tis of Thee 511

1. My coun-try, 'tis of thee, Sweet land of lib-er-ty,
2. My na-tive coun-try. thee, Land of the no-ble free,
3. Let mu-sic swell the breeze, And ring from all the trees
4. Our fa-thers' God, to thee, Au-thor of lib-er-ty,

Of thee I sing: Land where my fa-thers died, Land of the
Thy name I love: I love thy rocks and rills, Thy woods and
Sweet free-dom's song: Let mor-tal tongues a-wake; Let all that
To thee we sing: Long may our land be bright With free-dom's

pil-grims' pride, From ev-'ry moun-tain-side Let free-dom ring!
tem-pled hills; My heart with rap-ture thrills Like that a-bove.
breathe par-take; Let rocks their si-lence break, The sound pro-long.
ho-ly light; Pro-tect us by thy might, Great God, our King!

Words, Samuel F. Smith, 1831. Tune AMERICA, Anonymous.

Our Stewardship of the Earth

While driving one day, I passed a worn-out farm. Deep gullies were cut through the fields where the dirt had been washed away by the rains. The creek had been allowed to change its course in the bottom of the field and had cut out a new channel, ruining the good land in its way. Tall weeds and brambles were taking more strength from the soil already so poor that grass would scarcely grow.

With me as I viewed the place was a friend from Switzerland, and as he looked over the neglected farm, he exclaimed, "Oh, it is a crime! It is a crime to treat good land like that!"

The more I think about it, the more sure I am that he used the exact word to suit the case. It is a crime to wear out and ruin a farm, and the farmer who does so is a thief stealing from posterity. We are the heirs of the ages; but the estate is entailed, as large estates frequently are, so that while we inherit the earth, the great round world which is God's footstool, we have only the use of it while we live and must pass it on to those who come after us. We hold the property in trust and have no right to injure it or to lessen its value. To do so is dishonest, stealing from our heirs their inheritance.

The world is the beautiful estate of the human family passing down from generation to generation, marked by each holder while in his possession according to his character.

Did you ever think how a bit of land shows the character of the owner? A dishonest greed is shown by robbing the soil; the traits of a spendthrift are shown in wasting the resources of the farm by destroying its woods and waters, while carelessness and laziness are plainly to be seen in deep scars on the hillsides and washes in the lower fields.

> *For the earnest expectation of the creature waiteth for the manifestation of the sons of God. For the creature was made subject to vanity, not willingly, but by reason of him who hath subjected the same in hope, because the creature itself also shall be delivered from the bondage of corruption into the glorious liberty of the children of God. For we know that the whole creation groaneth and travaileth in pain together until now.*
>
> —ROMANS 8:19–22

It should be a matter of pride to keep our own farm, that little bit of the earth's surface for which we are responsible, in good condition, passing it on to our successor better than we found it. Trees should be growing where otherwise would be waste places, with the waters protected as much as possible from the hot sun and drying winds, with fields free from gullies and the soil fertile.

Beneficent Providence

We are inclined to think of Thanksgiving Day as a strictly American institution, and so, of course, it is in date and manner of celebration. But a harvest feast with the giving of praise and thanks to whatever gods were worshipped is a custom much older than our Thanksgiving that has been and still is observed by most races and peoples.

It seems to be instinctive for the human race to give thanks for benefits bestowed by a Higher Power. Some have worshipped the sun as the originator of blessings through its light and heat, while others have bowed the knee to lesser objects. Still, the feeling of gratitude in their hearts has been the same as we feel toward a beneficent providence who has given us the harvest as well as countless other blessings through the year. This is just another touch of nature that makes the whole world kin and links the present with the far distant past.

> *For I know the thoughts that I think toward you, saith the LORD, thoughts of peace, and not of evil, to give you an expected end. Then shall ye call upon me, and ye shall go and pray unto me, and I will hearken unto you.*
>
> —JEREMIAH 29:11–12

Mankind is not following a blind trail; feet were set upon the true path in the beginning. Following it at first by instinct, men stumbled from it often in the darkness of ignorance even as we do today, for we have much to learn. But even more than for material blessings, let us, with humble hearts, give thanks for the revelation [given] us and our better understanding of the greatness and goodness of God.

When Things Rule Mankind

Standing on the shore with the waves of the Pacific rolling to my feet, I looked over the waters as far as my eyes could reach until the gray of the ocean merged with the gray of the horizon's rim. One could not be distinguished from the other. Where, within my vision, the waters stopped and the skies began I could not tell, so softly they blended one into the other. The waves rolled in regularly, beating a rhythm of time, but the skies above them were unmeasured—so vast and far-reaching that the mind of man could not comprehend it.

A symbol of time and of eternity—time spaced by our counting into years, breaking at our feet as the waves break on the shore; and eternity, unmeasurable as the skies above us—blending one into the other at the farthest reach of our earthly vision.

As the New Year comes, seemingly with ever-increasing swiftness, there is a feeling that life is too short to accomplish the things we must do. But there is all eternity blending with the end of time for the things that really are worthwhile.

We are so overwhelmed with things these days that our lives are all more or less cluttered. I believe it is this, rather than a shortness of time, that gives us that feeling of hurry and almost of helplessness. Everyone is hurrying and usually just a little late. Notice the faces of the people who rush past on the streets or on our country roads! They nearly all have a strained, harassed look, and anyone you meet will tell you there is no time for anything anymore.

> *And one of the company said unto him, Master, speak to my brother, that he divide the inheritance with me. And he said unto him, Man, who made me a judge or a divider over you? And he said unto them, Take heed, and beware of covetousness: for a man's life consisteth not in the abundance of the things which he possesseth. And he spake a parable unto them, saying, The ground of a certain rich man brought forth plentifully: And he thought within himself, saying, What shall I do, because I have no room where to bestow my fruits? And he said, This will I do: I will pull down my barns, and build greater; and there will I bestow all my fruits and my goods. And I will say to my soul, Soul, thou hast much goods laid up for many years; take thine ease, eat, drink, and be merry. But God said unto him, Thou fool, this night thy soul shall be required of thee: then whose shall those things be, which thou has provided? So is he that layeth up treasure for himself, and is not rich toward God.*
> —LUKE 12:13–21

Life is so complicated! The day of the woman whose only needed tool was a hairpin is long since passed. But we might learn something from her and her methods even yet, for life would be pleasanter with some of the strain removed—if it were no longer true, as someone has said, that "things are in the saddle and rule mankind."

Here is a good New Year's resolution for us all to make: To simplify our lives as much as possible, to overcome that feeling of haste by remembering that there are just as many hours in the day as ever, and that there is time enough for the things that matter if time is rightly used.

Then, having done the most we may here, when we reach the limit of time, we will sail on over the horizon rim to new beauties and greater understanding.

Am I a Soldier of the Cross 388

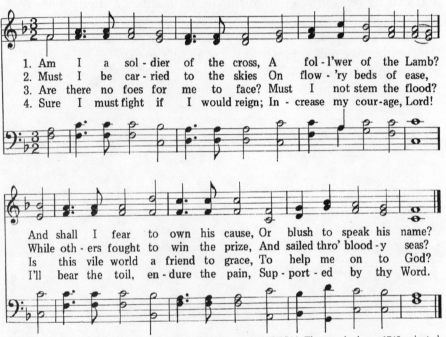

1. Am I a sol-dier of the cross, A fol-l'wer of the Lamb?
2. Must I be car-ried to the skies On flow-'ry beds of ease,
3. Are there no foes for me to face? Must I not stem the flood?
4. Sure I must fight if I would reign; In-crease my cour-age, Lord!

And shall I fear to own his cause, Or blush to speak his name?
While oth-ers fought to win the prize, And sailed thro' blood-y seas?
Is this vile world a friend to grace, To help me on to God?
I'll bear the toil, en-dure the pain, Sup-port-ed by thy Word.

1 Corinthians 16:13. Words, Isaac Watts, c. 1724. Tune ARLINGTON, Thomas A. Arne, 1762; adapted, Ralph Harrison, 1784.

Good Will unto Men

Peace upon earth the angel sang,
Good will unto men the chorus rang.

But that was many, many years ago at the first Christmas time. We could scarcely hear the angels if they were singing now for the clamor of disputing and wrangling that is going on where peace is supposed to be.

In our own country there is a gathering into groups with mutterings and threats of violence [1919], with some bloodshed and danger of more, and there is still war and threat of war over most of the world. This would be bad enough at any time, but just now, when we are thinking of all the blessed meanings of Christmastide, it becomes much more terrible.

A great deal is said and written about natural, national boundaries and learned discussions of racial antagonisms as causes of the restlessness and ill-temper of the nations; and there are investigations and commissions and inquiries to discover what is the matter with the world and to find a remedy.

> *And the angel said unto them, Fear not: for, behold, I bring you good tidings of great joy, which shall be to all people. For unto you is born this day in the city of David a Saviour, which is Christ the Lord. And this shall be a sign unto you; Ye shall find the babe wrapped in swaddling clothes, lying in a manger. And suddenly there was with the angel a multitude of the heavenly host praising God, and saying, Glory to God in the highest, and on earth peace, good will toward men.*
>
> —LUKE 2:10–14

But the cause of all the unrest and strife is easily found. It is selfishness, nothing else, selfishness deep in the hearts of people. It seems rather impossible that such a small thing as individual selfishness could cause so much trouble, but my selfishness added to your selfishness and that added to the selfishness of our neighbors all over the big, round world is not a small thing.

We may have thought that our own greed and striving to take unfair advantage were not noticed and never would be known, but you and I and our neighbors make the neighborhood and neighborhoods make the states and states make the nations and the nations are the peoples of the world.

No one would deny that the thoughts and actions and spirit of every person affect his neighborhood; and it is just as plain that the spirit and temper of the communities are reflected in the state and nation and influence the whole world.

The nations of Europe are selfishly trying to take advantage of one another in the settlement of boundaries and territory, and so the World War [WW 1] is like a fire that has been stopped in its wild advance only to smoulder and break out here and there a little farther back along the sides.

At home, in the troubles between labor and capital, each is willing to stop disputes and eager to cure the unrest of the people if it can be done at the expense of the other party and leave them undisturbed in their own selfish gains.

Following all the unrest and unreason on down to its real source where it lurks in the hearts of the people, its roots will be found there in individual selfishness, in the desire to better one's own condition at the expense of another by whatever means possible; and this desire of each person infects groups of people and moves nations.

Here and there one sees a criticism of Christianity because of the things that have happened and are still going on. "Christian civilization is a failure," some say. "Christianity has not prevented these things; therefore, it is a failure," say others.

But this is a calling of things by the wrong names. It is rather the lack of Christianity that has brought us where we are. Not a lack of churches or religious forms but of the real thing in our hearts.

There is no oppression of a group of people but has its root and inception in the hearts of the oppressors. There is no wild lawlessness and riot and bloodlust of a mob but has its place in the hearts of the persons who are that mob. Just so, if justice and fairness and kindness fill the minds of a crowd of persons, those things will be shown in their actions.

So, if we are eager to help in putting the world to rights, our first duty is to put ourselves right, to overcome our selfishness and be as eager that others shall be treated fairly as we are that no advantage shall be taken of ourselves; and to deal justly and have a loving charity and mercy for others as we wish them to have for us. Then we may hear the Christmas angels singing in our own hearts, "Peace upon earth! Good will unto men."

The Necessity of Work

There is good in everything, we are told, if we will only look for it; and I have at last found the good in a hard spell of illness. It is the same good the Irishman found in whipping himself.

"Why in the world are you doing that?" exclaimed the unexpected and astonished spectator.

"Because it feels so good when I stop," replied the Irishman with a grin. And this thing of being ill certainly does feel good when it stops. Why, even work looks good to a person who has been through such an enforced idleness, at least when strength is returning. Though I'll confess, if work crowds on me too soon, I am like the friend who was recovering from influenza rather more slowly than is usually the case.

"I eat all right and sleep all right," said he. "I even feel all right, but just the sight of a piece of work makes me tremble."

"That," said I, "is a terrible affliction, but I have known persons who suffer from it who never had the influenza."

> *And unto Adam he said, Because thou hast hearkened unto the voice of thy wife, and hast eaten of the tree, of which I commanded thee, saying, Thou shalt not eat of it: cursed is the ground for thy sake; in sorrow shalt thou eat of it all the days of thy life. Thorns also and thistles shall it bring forth to thee; and thou shalt eat the herb of the field; in the sweat of thy face shalt thou eat bread, till thou return unto the ground; for out of it wast thou taken: for dust thou art, and unto dust shalt thou return.*
>
> —GENESIS 3:17–19

But I'm sure we will all acknowledge that there is an advantage in having been ill if it makes us eager for work once more. Sometimes, I fancy we do not always appreciate the value of work and how dry and flavorless life would be without it.

If work were taken from us, we would lose rest also, for how could we rest unless we first became tired from working? Leisure would mean nothing to us for it would not be a prize to be won by effort and so would be valueless. Even play would lose its attraction for, if we played all the time, play would become tiresome; it would be nothing but work after all.

In that case, we would be at work again and perhaps a piece of actual work would become play to us. How topsy-turvy! But there is no cause for alarm. None of us is liable to be denied the pleasure of working, and that is good for us no one will deny. Man realized it soon after he was sentenced to "earn his bread by the sweat of his brow," and with his usual generosity he lost no time in letting his womenkind in on a good thing.

Keeping Friends

Sometimes we are a great trial to our friends and put an entirely uncalled-for strain upon our friendships by asking foolish questions.

The Man of the Place and I discovered the other day that we had for some time been saying to our friends, "Why don't you come over?" Can you think of a more awkward question than that? Just imagine the result if that question should always be answered truthfully. Some would reply, "Because I do not care to visit you." Others might say, "Because it is too much trouble," while still others who might care to come would be swamped in trying to enumerate the many little reasons why they had not done so. We decided that we would break ourselves of such a bad habit.

I once had a neighbor who, whenever we met, invariably asked me why I had not been to visit her. Even when I did go, she met me with the query, "Why haven't you been over before?" It was not a very pleasant greeting, and naturally one shuns unpleasantness when one may.

I have another neighbor who will call me on the phone and say: "It has been a long time since we have seen you, and we do want a good visit. Can't you come over tomorrow?" And immediately I wish to go. It does make such a difference how things are said.

> *Death and life are in the power of the tongue: and they*
> *that love it shall eat the fruit thereof. . . . A man that*
> *hath friends must shew himself friendly: and there is*
> *a friend that sticketh closer than a brother.*
> —PROVERBS 18:21, 24

Friendship is like love. It cannot be demanded or driven or insisted upon. It must be wooed to be won. The habit of saying disagreeable things, or of being careless about how what we say affects others, grows on us so easily and so surely if we indulge it.

"Mrs. Brown gave me an unhappy half hour a few days ago," said Mrs. Gray to me. "She said a great many unpleasant things and was generally disagreeable, but it is all right. The poor thing is getting childish, and we must overlook her oddities."

Mrs. Gray is a comparative newcomer in the neighborhood, but I have known Mrs. Brown for years; and ever since I have known her, she has prided herself on her plain speaking, showing very little regard for others' feelings. Her unkindness appears to me not a reversion to the mentality of childhood but simply an advance in the way she was going years ago. Her tongue has only become sharper with use, and her dexterity in hurting the feelings of others has grown with practice.

I know another woman of the same age whom no one speaks of as being childish. It is not necessary to make such an excuse for her because she is still, as she has been for twenty years, helpful and sweet and kind. And this helpfulness and sweetness and kindness of hers has grown with the passing years. I think no one will ever say of her, "Poor old thing, she is childish," as an excuse for her being disagreeable. I know she would hope to die before that time should come.

People do grow childish in extreme old age, of course, and should be treated with tenderness because of it; but I believe that even then the character which they have built during the years before will manifest itself. There is a great difference in children, you know, and I have come to the conclusion that if we live to reach a second childhood, we shall not be bad-tempered, disagreeable children unless we have indulged those traits.

Then there are the people who are "peculiar." Ever meet any of them?

The word seems to be less used than formerly, but there was a time when it was very common, and I longed to shriek everytime I heard it.

"Oh! You must not do that. George will be angry. He is so peculiar!"

"Of course, she doesn't belong with the rest of the crowd, but I had to invite her. She is so peculiar, you know, and so easily offended."

"I wouldn't pay any attention to that. Of course, she did treat you abominably, but it is just her way. She is so peculiar."

And so on and on. I thought seriously of cultivating a reputation for being peculiar, for like charity such a reputation seemed to cover multitudes of sins; but I decided that it would be even more unpleasant for me than for the other fellow; that it would not pay to make myself an unlovely character for the sake of any little, mean advantage to be gained by it.

Doing a Proper Accounting

We should bring ourselves to an accounting at the beginning of the New Year and ask these questions: What have I accomplished? Where have I fallen short of what I desired and planned to do and be?

I never have been in favor of making good resolutions on New Year's Day just because it was the first day of the year. Any day may begin a new year for us in that way, but it does help some to have a set time to go over the year's efforts and see whether we are advancing or falling back.

If we find that we are quicker of temper and sharper of tongue than we were a year ago, we are on the wrong road. If we have less sympathy and understanding for others and are more selfish than we used to be, it is time to take a new path.

> *Praise ye the LORD. I will praise the LORD with my whole heart, in the assembly of the upright, and in the congregation. The works of the LORD are great, sought out of all them that have pleasure therein. His work is honourable and glorious: and his righteousness endureth for ever. He hath made his wonderful works to be remembered: the LORD is gracious and full of compassion. He hath given meat unto them that fear him: he will ever be mindful of his covenant.*
> —PSALM 111:1–5

I helped a farmer figure out the value of his crops raised during the last season recently, and he was a very astonished person. Then when we added to that figure the amount he had received for livestock during the same period, he said: "It doesn't seem as if a man who had taken in that much off his farm would need a loan."

This farmer friend had not kept any accounts and so was surprised at the money he had taken in and that it should all be spent. Besides the help in a business way, there are a great many interesting things that can be gotten out of farm accounts if they are rightly kept.

The Man of the Place and I usually find out something new and unexpected when we figure up the business at the end of the year. We discovered this year that the two of us, without any outside help, had produced enough in the last year to feed thirty persons for a year—all the bread, butter, meat, eggs, sweetening, and vegetables necessary—and this does not include the beef cattle sold off the place.

So if you have not done so, just figure up for yourselves, and you will be surprised at how much you have accomplished.

"Thou Shalt Not Take the Name of the Lord Thy God in Vain"

I heard a boy swear the other day, and it gave me a distinctly different kind of shock than usual. I had just been reading an article in which our soldiers [of WW 1] were called crusaders who were offering themselves in their youth as a sacrifice in order that right might prevail against wrong and that those ideals, which are, in effect, the teachings of Christ, shall be accepted as the law of nations.

When I heard the boy use the name of Christ in an oath, I felt that he had belittled the mighty effort we are making, and that he had put an affront upon our brave soldiers by using lightly the name of the great Leader who first taught the principles for which they are dying. The boy had not thought of it in this way at all. He imagined that he was being very bold and witty, quite a grown man in fact.

> *Thou shalt not take the name of the* LORD *thy God in vain; for the* LORD *will not hold him guiltless that taketh his name in vain.*
>
> —EXODUS 20:7

I wonder how things came to be so reversed from the right order that it should be thought daring and smart to swear instead of being regarded as utterly foolish and a sign of weakness, betraying a lack of self-control. If people could only realize how ridiculous they appear when they call down the wrath of the Creator and Ruler of the Universe just because they have jammed their thumbs, I feel sure they would never be guilty of swearing again. It is so out of proportion, something as foolish and wasteful as it would be to use the long-range gun [a German artillery piece that could fire a shell seventy miles] which bombarded Paris to shoot a fly. If we call upon the Mightiest for trivial things, upon whom or what shall we call in the great moments of life?

There are some things in the world which should be damned to the nethermost regions, but surely it is not some frightened animal whom our own lack of self-control has made rebellious or an inanimate object that our own carelessness has caused to smite us. Language loses its value when it is so misapplied, and in moments of real and great stress or danger we have nothing left to say.

It is almost hopeless to try to reform older persons who have the habit of swearing fastened upon them. Like any other habit, it is difficult to break, and it is useless to explain to them that it is a waste of force and nervous energy. But I think we should show children the absurdity of wasting the big shells of language on small insignificant objects.

Perhaps a little ridicule might prick that bubble of conceit, and the boy with his mouth full of his first oaths might not feel himself such a dashing, daredevil of a fellow if he feared that he had made himself ridiculous.

Gossiping

Did you ever chase thistledown? Oh, of course, when you were a child, but I mean since you have been grown! Some of us should be chasing thistledown a good share of the time.

There is an old story, for the truth of which I cannot vouch, which is so good that I am going to take the risk of telling it; and if any of you have heard it before, it will do no harm to recall it to your minds.

A woman once confessed to the priest that she had been gossiping. To her surprise, the priest instructed her to go gather a ripe head of the thistle and scatter the seed on the wind, then to return to him. This she did, wondering why she had been told to do so strange a thing; but her penance was only begun, for when she returned to the priest, instead of forgiving her fault, he said: "The thistledown is scattered as were your idle words. My daughter, go and gather up the thistledown!"

He that keepeth his mouth keepeth his life: but he that openeth wide his lips shall have destruction.
—PROVERBS 13:3

It is so easy to be careless and one is so prone to be thoughtless in talking. I told only half of a story the other day heedlessly over-looking the fact that by telling only a part, I left the listeners with a wrong impression of some very kindly persons. Fortunately, I saw in time what I had done, and I pounced on that thistledown before the wind caught it or else I should have had a chase.

A newcomer in the neighborhood says, "I do like Mrs. Smith! She seems such a fine woman."

"Well, y-e-s," we reply, "I've known her a long time," and we leave the new acquaintance wondering what it is we know against Mrs. Smith. We have said nothing against her, but we have "damned her with faint praise" and a thistle seed is sown on the wind.

The noun "gossip" is not of the feminine gender. No, absolutely not! A man once complained to me of some things that had been said about his wife. "Damn these gossiping women!" he exclaimed. "They do nothing but talk about their neighbors who are better than they. Mrs. Cook spends her time running around gossiping when she should be taking care of her children. Poor things, they never have enough to eat by their looks. Her housework is never done, and as for her character, everybody knows about—" and he launched into a detailed account of an occurrence which certainly sounded very compromising as he told it. I repeated to myself his first remark with the word "men" in place of the word "women" just to see how it would sound.

And so we say harmful things carelessly; we say unkind things in a spirit of retaliation or in a measure of self-defense to prove that we are no worse than others, and the breeze of idle chatter from many tongues picks them up, blows them here and there, and scatters them to the four corners of the earth. What a crop of thistles they raise! If we were obliged to go gather up the seed before it had time to grow as the woman in the story was told to do, I am afraid we would be even busier than we are.

Early Training

"Don't open that door again, Tom! It lets in too much cold," said Tom's mother with what I thought was an unnecessarily sharp note in her voice.

It was the first chilly day of early autumn, and there was no fire in the house except in the kitchen stove. As I was making an afternoon visit, we, of course, sat in the front room—and shivered. In a moment, the outside door opened again and Tom and a gust of raw wind entered together.

"I told you not to open that door! If you do it again, I'll spank you good!" said Tom's mother, and Tom immediately turned around, opened the door and went out.

We talked on busily for another moment when, feeling more chilly than usual, I looked around and saw Tom standing in the open door, swinging it to and fro.

"Tom!" exclaimed his mother, "I told you not to open that door! Come here to me!" As the door swung shut, Tom turned and faced his mother, took a few steps toward her, raised himself on his tiptoes, with his hands behind him—and turned around, opened the door, and walked out.

His mother screamed after him, "Tom! If you open that door again, I'll skin you alive!"

"You know you wouldn't do that, and Tom knows it too," I said.

"Oh, of course," she replied, "but I have to tell him something."

Train up a child in the way he should go: and when he is old, he will not depart from it.
—PROVERBS 22:6

I know Tom's mother is trying to teach her boy to be truthful; but a few days ago, he got into mischief, and when asked who had done the damage he replied, "Sister did it."

Tom was punished for telling a lie, but I imagine it would be rather difficult to explain to him why it was all right to tell a falsehood about what would happen and all wrong to tell one about what had happened; why he should be punished and his mother not.

While I was busy with my work the other morning, a great commotion arose in the dooryard. There was shouting, the dog was barking furiously, and there was the noise of running and trampling. I hurried to the door and found several boys in the yard darting here and there, shouting to each other, "Catch it! There it goes!"

As I opened the door, a couple of the boys put their feet into the meshes of the woven wire fence and climbed over it as though it had been a stairs, although the gate was only a few steps from them. Evidently, that was the way they had entered the dooryard.

"Boys, what are you doing?" I asked. "Oh! Just chasing butterflies," answered one, while another added as though that excused everything, "Our teacher is just down there," indicating a place well within the fenced field.

When we had taken stock of the damage done by the butterfly chasers, we found that the barbed wire fence had been broken down where they had entered the fields, and the woven wire fence was badly stretched and sagged. Wire fencing is high these days and help impossible to get so that such raids are particularly annoying just now though they are not by any means anything new.

We are engaged just now in a mighty struggle to teach a certain part of the people of the world a respect for truth and for the rights and property of other people. Are we failing to teach these things at home as we should?

Truly, "As the twig is bent, the tree inclines."

Nice Discernment

"You have so much tact and can get along with people so well," said a friend to me once. Then, after a thoughtful pause, she added, "But I never could see any difference between tact and trickery." Upon my assuring her that there was no difference, she pursued the subject further.

"Now I have no tact whatever, but speak plainly," she said pridefully. "The Scotch people are, I think, the most tactful, and the Scotch, you know, are the trickiest nation in the world."

As I am of Scotch descent, I could restrain my merriment no longer, and when I recovered enough to say, "You are right, I am Scotch," she smiled ruefully and said, "I told you I had no tact."

Tact does for life just what lubricating oil does for machinery. It makes the wheels run smoothly, and without it there is a great deal of friction and the possibility of a breakdown. Many a car on the way of life fails to make the trip as expected for lack of this lubricant.

> *But the tongue can no man tame; it is an unruly evil, full of deadly poison. Therewith bless we God, even the Father; and therewith curse we men, which are made after the similitude of God. Out of the same mouth proceedeth blessing and cursing. My brethren, these things ought not so to be. Doth a fountain send forth at the same place sweet water and bitter? Can the fig tree, my brethren, bear olive berries? either a vine, figs? so can no fountain both yield salt water and fresh. Who is a wise man and endued with knowledge among you? let him shew out of a good conversation his works with meekness of wisdom.*
> —JAMES 3:8–13

Tact is a quality that may be acquired. It is only the other way of seeing and presenting a subject. There are always two sides to a thing, you know; and if one side is disagreeable, the reverse is quite apt to be very pleasant. The tactful person may see both sides but uses the pleasant one.

"Your teeth are so pretty when you keep them white," said Ida to Stella, which, of course, was equal to saying that Stella's teeth were ugly when she did not keep them clean, as frequently happened; but Stella left her friend with the feeling that she had been complimented and also with the shamed resolve that she would keep those pretty teeth white.

Tom's shoulders were becoming inclined to droop a little. To be sure, he was a little older than he used to be and sometimes very tired, but the droop was really caused more by carelessness than by anything else. When Jane came home from a visit to a friend whose husband was very round-shouldered indeed, she noticed more plainly than usual the beginning of the habit in Tom.

Choosing a moment when he straightened to his full height and squared his shoulders, she said: "Oh, Tom! I'm so glad you are tall and straight, not round-shouldered like Dick. He is growing worse every day until it is becoming a positive deformity with him." And Tom was glad she had not observed the tendency in his shoulders, and thereafter their straightness was noticeable.

Jane might have chosen a moment when Tom's shoulders were drooping and with perfect truthfulness have said: "Tom! You are getting to be round-shouldered and ugly like Dick. In a little while you will look like a hunchback."

Tom would have felt hurt and resentful and probably would have retorted, "Well, you're getting older and uglier too," or something like that; and his hurt pride and vanity would have been a hindrance instead of a help to improvement.

The children, of course, get their bad tempers from their fathers, but I think we get our vanity from Adam, for we all have it, men and women alike; and like most things it is good when rightly used.

Tact may be trickery, but after all I think I prefer the dictionary definition—"nice discernment." To be tactful, one has only to discern or distinguish or, in other words, to see nicely and speak and act accordingly.

My sympathy just now, however, is very much with the persons who seem to be unable to say the right thing at the proper time. In spite of oneself there are times when one's mental fingers seem to be all thumbs. At a little gathering not long ago, I differed with the hostess on a question which arose and disagreed with just a shade more warmth than I intended. I resolved to make it up by being a little extra sweet to her before I left.

The refreshments served were so dainty and delicious that I thought I would find some pleasant way to tell her so. But alas! As it was a very hot day, ice water was served after the little luncheon, and I found myself looking sweetly into my hostess's face and heard myself say, "Oh, wasn't that water good." What could one do after that, but murmur the conventional, "Such a pleasant afternoon," at leaving and depart feeling like a little girl who had blundered at her first party.

Difficulties

"A difficulty raiseth the spirit of a great man. He hath a mind to wrestle with it and give it a fall. A man's mind must be very low if the difficulty doth not make part of his pleasure." By the test of these words of Lord Halifax, there are a number of great persons in the world today.

After all, what is a difficulty but a direct challenge? "Here I am in your way," it says, "you cannot get around me nor overcome me! I have blocked your path!" Anyone of spirit will accept the challenge and find some way to get around or over or through that obstacle. Yes! And find pleasure in the difficulty for the sheer joy of surmounting it as well as because there has been an opportunity once more to prove one's strength and cunning and, by the very use of these qualities, cause an increase of them.

The overcoming of one difficulty makes easier the conquering of the next until finally we are almost invincible. Success actually becomes a habit through the determined overcoming of obstacles as we meet them one by one.

If we are not being successful, if we are more or less on the road toward failure, a change in our fortunes can be brought by making a start, however small, in the right direction and then following it up. We can form the habit of success by beginning with some project and putting it through to a successful conclusion, however long and hard we must fight to do so, by "wrestling with" one difficulty and "giving it a fall." The next time it will be easier.

> *But watch thou in all things, endure afflictions, do the work of an evangelist, make full proof of thy ministry. For I am now ready to be offered, and the time of my departure is at hand. I have fought a good fight, I have finished my course, I have kept the faith: henceforth there is laid up for me a crown of righteousness, which the Lord, the righteous judge, shall give me at that day: and not to me only, but unto all them also that love his appearing.*
>
> —2 TIMOTHY 4:5–8

For some reason, of course, according to some universal law, we gather momentum as we proceed in whatever way we go; and just as by overcoming a small difficulty, we are more able to conquer the next, though greater; so if we allow ourselves to fail, it is easier to fail the next time, and failure becomes a habit until we are unable to look a difficulty fairly in the face, but turn and run from it.

There is no elation equal to the rise of the spirit to meet and overcome a difficulty, not with a foolish overconfidence but by keeping things in their proper relations by praying, now and then, the prayer of a good fighter whom I used to know: "Lord, make me sufficient to mine own occasion."

Always Be Ready

Did the first frost catch you unready? It would be quite unusual if it didn't because I never knew anyone to be ready for cold weather in the fall or for the first warm spell in the spring. It is like choosing the right time to be ill or like choosing an out-of-the-way place for a boil—it simply isn't done!

I know a man who had a little patch of corn. He was not quite ready to cut it and, besides, he said, "It is just a little green." He let it wait until the frost struck it, and now he says it is too dry and not worth cutting. The frost saved him a lot of hard work.

This man's disposition reminds me of that of a renter we once had who was unable to plow the corn in all summer. Before it rained the ground was so hard he could not keep the plow in; and, besides, if it did not rain, there would be no corn anyway, and he believed it was going to be a dry season. When it did rain, it was too wet to plow, and never was he ready and able to catch that cornfield when the ground was right for plowing.

> *Watch therefore: for ye know not what hour your Lord doth come. But know this, that if the goodman of the house had known in what watch the thief would come, he would have watched, and would not have suffered his house to be broken up. Therefore be ye also ready: for in such an hour as ye think not the Son of man cometh. Who then is a faithful and wise servant, whom his lord hath made ruler over his household, to give them meat in due season? Blessed is that servant, whom his lord when he cometh shall find so doing.*
>
> —MATTHEW 24:42–46

And that reminds me of the other renter who was always ready to take advantage of his opportunities. His horses would break into the cornfield at night, or were turned in (we never knew which), and in the fall when the Man of the Place wanted a share of what corn was left, he was told that the horses had eaten all his share.

These anecdotes are not intended as any reflection on renters. I could tell some in which the joke is on the other side if I had the space.

The tragedy of being unready is easy to find, for more often than not success or failure turn upon just that one thing. There was a time, perhaps long ago, when you were not ready for examinations and failed to pass; then there was the time you were not ready to make that good investment because you had been spending carelessly. We can all remember many times when we were not ready. While being ready for and equal to whatever comes may be in some sense a natural qualification, it is a characteristic that may be cultivated, especially if we learn easily by experience.

It was interesting to see the way different persons showed their character after the first frost. One man considered that the frost had done his work for him and so relieved him of further effort. Others went along at their usual gait and saved their fodder in a damaged condition. They had done the best they could, let providence take the responsibility. Still others worked through the moonlight nights and saved their feed in good condition in spite of the frost. They figured that it "was up to them" and no little thing like the first frost should spoil their calculations.

It does not so much matter what happens. It is what one does when it happens that really counts.

206 I Will Sing You A Song

ELLEN H. GATES

PHILIP PHILLIPS

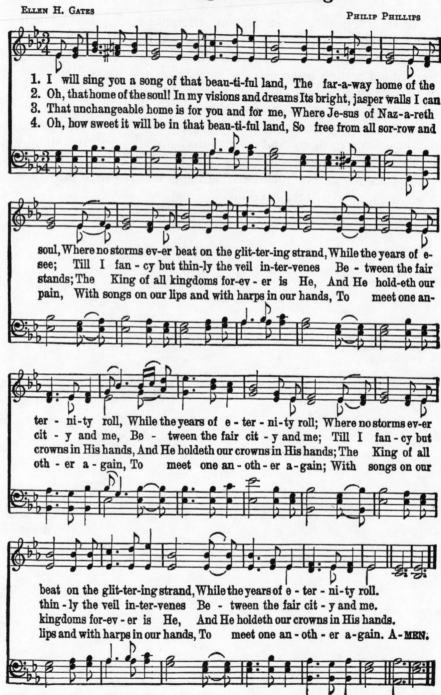

1. I will sing you a song of that beau-ti-ful land, The far-a-way home of the
2. Oh, that home of the soul! In my visions and dreams Its bright, jasper walls I can
3. That unchangeable home is for you and for me, Where Je-sus of Naz-a-reth
4. Oh, how sweet it will be in that beau-ti-ful land, So free from all sor-row and

soul, Where no storms ev-er beat on the glit-ter-ing strand, While the years of e-
see; Till I fan - cy but thin-ly the veil in-ter-venes Be - tween the fair
stands; The King of all kingdoms for-ev - er is He, And He hold-eth our
pain, With songs on our lips and with harps in our hands, To meet one an-

ter - ni-ty roll, While the years of e - ter - ni-ty roll; Where no storms ev-er
cit - y and me, Be - tween the fair cit - y and me; Till I fan - cy but
crowns in His hands, And He holdeth our crowns in His hands; The King of all
oth - er a - gain, To meet one an - oth-er a-gain; With songs on our

beat on the glit-ter-ing strand, While the years of e - ter - ni-ty roll.
thin - ly the veil in-ter-venes Be - tween the fair cit - y and me.
kingdoms for-ev - er is He, And He holdeth our crowns in His hands.
lips and with harps in our hands, To meet one an - oth - er a-gain. A-MEN.

The Lord Gives the Increase

The Man of the Place was worried about the weather. He said the indications were for a dry season, and ever since I have been remembering droughts. There were dry years in the Dakotas when we were beginning our life together. How heartbreaking it was to watch the grain we had sown with such high hopes wither and turn yellow in the hot winds! And it was backbreaking as well as heartbreaking to carry water from the well to my garden and see it dry up despite all my efforts.

I said at that time that thereafter I would sow the seed, but the Lord would give the increase if there was any, for I could not do my work and that of Providence also by sending the rain on the gardens of the just or the unjust.

*Consider the lilies of the field, how they grow; they toil
not, neither do they spin: and yet I say unto you, That
even Solomon in all his glory was not arrayed like one
of these. Wherefore, if God so clothe the grass of the field,
which to day is, and to morrow is cast into the oven,
shall he not much more clothe you, O ye of little faith?*
—MATTHEW 6:28b–30

But still I suppose our brains were given us to use by the same
Providence that created the laws of nature, and what we accomplish
by the use of them is, in a certain sense, its work. Just as all good is for
us if we but reach out our hand to take it, so in the higher atmosphere
around our earth there is a great supply of moisture. It is there for our
use if, with the brains which God has given us, we can find a way to
tap it. This is what a California man claims to have done [in 1924].

Hatfield, the rainmaker, lives in Glendale, California, near Los
Angeles. He claims to be able to make rain by projecting into the
atmosphere, from a high scaffolding, certain chemicals that attract
and precipitate moisture. There are always storms in movement, and
storm formations pass high over a country without ever condensing
and causing rain. The way he operates, he'll make that storm give up
its water as it comes along.

In 1915 there was a very severe drought in southern California,
especially in San Diego County where the water situation became
critical. As a last resort, the San Diego Chamber of Commerce decided
to try out this man Hatfield. A contract was made by which he was to
receive $10,000 if he brought down water enough to fill the great irri-
gation reservoir. Shortly after he began operations, the rain began to
fall in such quantities that the reservoir not only filled but burst its
dam, and the Chamber of Commerce, instead of paying him $10,000,
brought suit against him for damages in destroying the dam.

*Take therefore no thought for the morrow: for the mor-
row shall take thought for the things of itself. Sufficient
unto the day is the evil thereof.*
—MATTHEW 6:34

The Preaching Farmer

There is at least one Missourian who is not asking to be "shown" [Missouri is the "Show Me" state]. A. C. Barton of Show You Farm says Missouri people have said "show me" long enough, and they should now say "I will show you," which he is proceeding to do.

Mr. Barton used to be a Methodist preacher. He says that no one ever accused him of being the best preacher at the St. Louis conference, but they did all acknowledge that he was the best farmer among them. He thought perhaps he had made a mistake like the man who saw, in a vision, the letters G. P. C. and thought he had a call to preach, the letters standing for "Go Preach Christ."

Later he decided that the letters meant "Go Plow Corn," so Mr. Barton made up his mind to follow the profession in which he excelled. He came to Mountain Grove [Missouri] from Dallas County, Nebraska, eight years ago.

> *Ye are the light of the world. A city that is set on an hill cannot be hid. Neither do men light a candle, and put it under a bushel, but on a candlestick; and it giveth light unto all that are in the house. Let your light so shine before men, that they may see your good works, and glorify your Father which is in heaven.*
> —MATTHEW 5:14–16

While waiting for his train in Kansas City, Mr. Barton noticed a man, also waiting, surrounded by bundles and luggage. For some reason Mr. Barton thought he was from the Ozarks and approaching him asked:

"Are you from Missouri?"

"Yes sir," answered the man.

"From the Ozarks?" Mr. Barton inquired.

"Yes sir," answered the man.

"Are there any farms for sale down there where you came from?" Mr. Barton asked.

"Yes sir. They're all for sale," replied the man from the Ozarks.

While that might have been true at the time, it would not be true now, for Show You Farm is not for sale.

When Mr. Barton bought his 80-acre farm on the "post oak flats" near Mountain Grove, the people he met gave him the encouragement usually given the new comers in the Ozarks. They told him the land was good for nothing, that he could not raise anything on it.

One man remarked in his hearing, "These new comers are workers," and another replied: "They'll have to work if they make a living on that place. Nobody's ever done it yet."

They soon found that there was more work on an 80-acre farm than they could handle, for while there were eight in the family, the six children were small, so it was decided to adjust the work to the family and 40 acres of the land, on which were the improvements, were sold for $2,500. Later 15 acres more were sold for $600. As the place had cost only $40 an acre, that left only $100 as the cost of the 25-acre farm that was kept.

These 25 acres of unimproved, poor land have been made into a truly remarkable little farm. During last season, it produced the following crops: 10 acres of corn, 400 bushels; 2 acres of oats, 20 bushels; 1 acre of millet hay, 2 tons; 1 acre of sorghum, 115 gallons of molasses; cowpeas, 100 bushels.

Besides these crops there was a 5-acre truck [garden] patch which furnished a good income thru the summer, but of which no account was kept. There has been sold off the place this last season livestock amounting to $130, poultry $15, butter $250, and grain $35. The rest of the grain was still on the place when this was written. Not bad for a 25-acre farm, is it?

As there is a young orchard of 3 acres, a pasture and necessarily some ground used for building sites, you may wonder where the cowpeas were raised. Mr. Barton plants cowpeas with all other crops. He says it is the surest, quickest, and cheapest way to build up the soil. When garden crops are harvested, cowpeas are planted in their place. They follow the oats and rye and are planted with the corn.

There never has been a pound of commercial fertilizer used on Show You Farm. When clearing his land, Mr. Barton traded wood for stable manure in the town, so that he paid, with his labor, for 300 tons of stable fertilizer. Except for this, the soil has been built up by rotation of crops and raising of cowpeas, until from a complete failure of the corn crop the first year, because of poverty of the soil, last year's bountiful crops were harvested.

By the good farming methods of the Barton family they made their land bring them an average of $30 an acre even in the last dry seasons.

Mr. Barton believes in cultivation, both with plows and by hand. He is old fashioned enough to hoe his corn. A neighbor passing and seeing him hoeing said, "If I can't raise corn without hoeing it, I won't raise it," and he didn't for it was a dry season.

As Mr. Barton says, "The reason there are so many POOR farmers is because there are so many poor FARMERS.

It is not all work and money making at the Barton home, however. In strawberry time the Sunday school is invited out and treated to strawberries with cream and sugar. Last season it took 8 gallons of strawberries to supply the feast. When melons are ripe, there is another gathering and sometimes as many as 100 persons enjoy the delicious treat.

In the long winter evenings, work and pleasure are mixed and while one of the family reads aloud some interesting book, the others shell the cowpeas that have been gathered in the fall.

Mr. Barton has not been allowed to drop all his outside activities. He has been elected secretary of the Farmers Mutual Fire Insurance Company and is helping them to organize for their mutual benefit. Also his services are often in demand to supply a country pulpit here and there, for once a Methodist preacher, a man is always more or less a Methodist preacher; and as Mr. Barton goes on his daily way, both by acts and words, he is preaching kindness, helpfulness, and the brotherhood of man.

He also preaches an agricultural theology. He says that robbing the soil is sin, and that like every other sin it brings its own punishment.

That Mr. Barton has not committed that sin, the greatest agricultural sin, one is assured when looking over the farm; and what he has accomplished is certainly encouraging for the man with a bit of poor land. Mr. Barton's advice to such a man is "not to go looking for a better place but MAKE one."

Redeeming the Time

Spring has come! The wild birds have been singing the glad tidings for several days, but they are such optimistic little souls that I always take their songs of spring with a grain of pessimism. The squirrels and chipmunks have been chattering to me, telling the same news, but they are such cheerful busybodies that I never believe quite all they say.

But now I know that spring is here, for as I passed the little creek on my way to the mailbox this morning, I saw scattered papers caught on the bushes, empty cracker and sandwich cartons strewn around on the green grass, and discolored pasteboard boxes soaking in the clear water of the spring.

> *See then that ye walk circumspectly, not as fools, but*
> *as wise, redeeming the time, because the days are evil.*
> —EPHESIANS 5:15–16

I knew then that spring was here, for the sign of the picnickers is more sure than that of singing birds and tender green grass, and there is nothing more unlovely than one of nature's beauty spots defiled in this way. It is such an unprovoked offense to nature, something like insulting one's host after enjoying his hospitality. It takes just a moment to put back into the basket the empty boxes and paper, and one can depart gracefully leaving the place all clean and beautiful for the next time or the next party.

Did you ever arrive all clean and fresh, on a beautiful summer morning, at a pretty picnic place and find that someone had been before you, and that the place was all littered up with dirty papers and buzzing flies? If you have and have ever left a place in the same condition, it served you right. Let's keep the open spaces clean, not fill them up with rubbish!

It is so easy to get things cluttered up—one's days, for instance, as well as picnic places—to fill them with empty, useless things and so make them unlovely and tiresome. Even though the things with which we fill our days were once important, if they are serving no good purpose now, they have become trash like the empty boxes and papers of the picnickers. It will pay to clean this trash away and keep our days as uncluttered as possible.

There are just now so many things that must be done that we are tempted to spend ourselves recklessly, especially as it is rather difficult to decide what to eliminate; and we cannot possibly accomplish everything. We must continually be weighing and judging and discarding things that are presented to us if we would save ourselves and spend our time and strength only on those things that are important. We may be called upon to spend our health and strength to the last bit, but we should see to it that we do not waste them. [WW 1 priorities were making themselves felt to Ozark patriots.]

"Oh, I am so tired that I just want to sit down and cry," a friend confided to me, "and here is the club meeting on hand and the lodge practice and the Red Cross workday and the aid society meeting and the church bazaar to get ready for, to say nothing of the pie supper at the schoolhouse and the spring sewing and garden and—Oh! I don't see how I'm ever going to get through it all!"

Of course, she was a little hysterical. It didn't all have to be done at once, but it showed how over-tired she was, and it was plain that something must give way—if nothing else, herself. My friend needed a little open space in her life.

We must none of us shirk. We must do our part in every way, but let's be sure we clear away the rubbish, that we do nothing for empty form's sake nor because someone else does, unless it is the thing that should be done.

How Is It with You, Friend?

Heartache, rather than contentment and happiness, has been the lot of a friend of ours who failed to recognize the inalienable right of a child to have something of his very own.

Children, obey your parents in the Lord: for this is right. Honour thy father and mother; (which is the first commandment with promise;) that it may be well with thee, and thou mayest live long on the earth. And, ye fathers, provoke not your children to wrath: but bring them up in the nurture and admonition of the Lord.
—EPHESIANS 6:1–4

Reared on one of the best farms in Missouri, the son of the house, as he grew into manhood, resented the fact that no matter how hard he labored nor how prosperous the season the day never came when he could call a dime his own. Always it was, "Dad, can I have money for a pair of shoes?" or "Dad, I'd like to go to the picnic tomorrow. Can I have 50 cents to spend?" Grudgingly was the money given; always was there the insistent demand for an accounting of every cent. "Someday, son," he'd say, "I'm going to give you a farm. Got to count the pennies and work hard."

Came the day when the boy was a man and demands were made for a fixed sum. "Give me even 50 cents a day, Dad," he said, "when you pay the hired men $2.50, and I'll be satisfied." But the father turned a deaf ear and a stony heart to the appeal, and so the boy left home to win his way among strangers.

Embittered is the father, sorrowful the mother, and only He who looks down into the hearts of men may know the hunger that fills each heart as they go their separate ways. How is it with you, friend?

A Longing Unutterable Fills My Heart

A letter from my mother, who is seventy-six years old, lies on my desk beside a letter from my daughter far away in Europe. Reading the message from my mother, I am a child again and a longing unutterable fills my heart for Mother's counsel, for the safe haven of her protection and the relief from responsibility which trusting in her judgment always gave me.

But when I turn to the letter written by my daughter, who will always be a little girl to me no matter how old she grows, then I understand and appreciate my mother's position and her feelings toward me.

Many of us have the blessed privilege of being at the same time mother and child, able to let the one interpret the other to us until our understanding of both is full and rich. What is there in the attitude of your children toward yourself that you wish were different? Search your heart and learn if your ways toward your own mother could be improved.

> *Honour thy father and thy mother: that thy days may be long upon the land which the* Lord *thy God giveth thee.*
>
> —EXODUS 20:12

In the light of experience and the test of the years, can you see how your mother might have been more to you, could have guided you better? Then be sure you are making the most of your privileges with the children who are looking to you for love and guidance. For there is, after all, no great difference between the generations; the problems of today and tomorrow must be met in much the same way as those of yesterday.

During the years since my mother was a girl to the time when my daughter was a woman, there have been many slight, external changes in the fashions and ways of living, some change in the thought of the world, and much more freedom in expressing those thoughts. But the love of mother and child is the same, with the responsibility of controlling and guiding on the one side and the obligation of obedience and respect on the other.

The most universal sentiment in the world is that of mother-love. From the highest to the lowest in the scale of humanity, and all through the animal kingdom, it is the strongest force in creation, the conserver of life, the safeguard of evolution. It holds within its sheltering care the fulfillment of the purpose of creation itself. In all ages, in all countries it is the same—a boundless, all-enveloping love; if necessary, a sacrifice of self for the offspring.

Think of the number of children in the world, each the joy of some mother's heart, each a link connecting one generation with another, each a hope for the future. . . .

It stuns the mind to contemplate their number and their possibilities, for these are the coming rulers of the world: the makers of destiny, not only for their own generation but for the generations to come. And they are being trained for their part in the procession of time by the women of today. Surely, "The hand that rocks the cradle is the hand that rules the world."

Thoughts on Being a Neighbor

There are two vacant places in our neighborhood. Two neighbors have gone ahead on "the great adventure."

We become so accustomed to our neighbors and friends that we take their presence as a matter of course, forgetting that the time in which we may enjoy their companionship is limited, and when they are no longer in their places, there is always a little shock of surprise mingled with our grief.

When we came to the Ozarks more than twenty years ago [1894], neighbor Deaver was one of the first to welcome us to our new home, and now he has moved on ahead to that far country from which no trav-eler returns. Speaking of Mrs. Case's illness and death, a young woman said, "I could not do much to help them, but I did what I could, for Mrs. Case was mighty good to me when I was sick." That tells the story. The neighborhood will miss them both for they were good neighbors. What remains to be said? What greater praise could be given?

I wonder if you all know the story of the man who was moving from one place to another because he had such bad neighbors. Just before making the change, he met a man from the neighborhood to which he was going and told him in detail how mean his old neigh-bors were, so bad in fact that he would not live among them any longer. Then he asked the other man what the neighbors were like in the place to which he was moving. The other man replied, "You will find just the same kind of neighbors where you are going as those you leave behind you."

> *And, behold, a certain lawyer stood up, and tempted him, saying, Master, what shall I do to inherit eternal life? He said unto him, What is written in the law? how readest thou? And he answering said, Thou shalt love the Lord thy God with all thy heart, and with all thy soul, and with all thy strength, and with all thy mind: and thy neighbour as thyself. And he said unto him, Thou hast answered right: this do, and thou shalt live.*
> —LUKE 10:25–28

It is true that we find ourselves reflected in our friends and neigh-bors to a surprising extent, and if we are in the habit of having bad neighbors, we are not likely to find better by changing our location. We might as well make good neighbors in our own neighborhood, beginning, as they tell us charity should, at home.

If we make good neighbors of ourselves, we likely shall not need to seek new friends in strange places. This would be a tiresome world if everyone were shaped to a pattern of our own cutting, and I think we enjoy our neighbors more if we accept them just as they are.

Sometimes it is rather hard to do, for certainly it takes all kinds of neighbors to make a community. We once had a neighbor who borrowed nearly everything on the place. Mr. Skelton was a good borrower but a very poor hand to return anything. As he lived just across a narrow road from us, it was very convenient—for him. He borrowed the hand tools and the farm machinery, the grindstone and the whetstone, and the harness and saddles, also groceries and kitchen tools.

One day he came over and borrowed my wash boiler in which to heat water for butchering. In a few minutes he returned, and making a separate trip for each article, he borrowed both my dishpans, my two butcher knives, the knife sharpener, a couple of buckets, the boards on which to lay the hog, some matches to light his fire, and as an afterthought while the water was heating, he came for some salt. There was a fat hog in our pen, and I half expected him to come back once more and borrow the hog, but luckily he had a hog of his own. A few days later when I asked to borrow a paper, I was told that they never lent their papers. And yet this family were kind neighbors later when we really needed their help.

The Smiths moved in from another state. Their first caller was informed that they did not want the neighbors "to come about them at all," didn't want to be bothered with them. No one knew the reason, but all respected their wishes and left them alone. As he was new to the country, Mr. Smith did not make a success of his farming, but he was not bothered with friendly advice either.

There's a Land That Is Fairer Than Day 471

SWEET BY AND BY. 9. 9. 9. 9. with Refrain

SANFORD F. BENNETT, 1836-1898   JOSEPH P. WEBSTER, 1819-1875

1. There's a land that is fair-er than day, And by faith we can see it a-far; For the Fa-ther waits o-ver the way To pre-pare us a dwell-ing place there.

2. We shall sing on that beau-ti-ful shore The me-lo-di-ous songs of the blest, And our spir-its shall sor-row no more, Not a sigh for the bless-ing of rest.

3. To our boun-ti-ful Fa-ther a-bove, We will of-fer the trib-ute of praise For the glo-ri-ous gift of His love And the bless-ings that hal-low our days.

REFRAIN

In the sweet by and by, We shall meet on that beau-ti-ful shore; In the sweet by and by, We shall meet on that beau-ti-ful shore.

in the sweet by and by, by and by;

In the sweet by and by,

Mother

"Mother passed away morning" [Caroline Quiner Ingalls, "Ma" Ingalls, 1839–1924] was the message that came over the wires, and a darkness overshadowed the spring sunshine; a sadness crept into the birds' songs.

Some of us have received such messages. Those who have not, one day will. Just as when a child, home was lonely when Mother was gone, so to children of a larger growth, the world seems a lonesome place when Mother has passed away and only memories of her are left us—happy memories if we have not given ourselves any cause for regret.

Saving Graces

> _Weeping may endure for a night, but joy cometh in the morning._
>
> —Psalm 30:5b

Memories! We go through life collecting them whether we will or not! Sometimes I wonder if they are our treasures in Heaven or the consuming fires of torment when we carry them with us as we, too, pass on.

What a joy our memories may be or what a sorrow! But glad or sad they are with us forever. Let us make them carefully of all good things, rejoicing in the wonderful truth that while we are laying up for ourselves the very sweetest and best of happy memories, we are at the same time giving them to others.

164